"Biblical. Crisp. Fast pa
sessment of, and remedy foi
referred to as New England. .   ... a theological and historical primer written from the perspective of a passionate insider. As you read this book, you can feel Nate's heart burn for the salvation of souls and the Lord's glory in the veritable graveyard of Christianity. Whether you want the Lord to revive the hearts of people in New England, or in your hometown, *Reviving* lays out the biblical elixir for God-honoring change. Maybe Gilmanton, New Hampshire will be famous for three things one day?"

—MIKE ABENDROTH, Pastor of Bethlehem Bible Church, West Boylston, MA and host of No Compromise Radio.

"Nate Pickowicz has provided an insightful diagnosis of what ills New England churches. He has also provided a potent antidote—revival; the sort of revival that took New England by storm in the mid-eighteenth century known as the Great Awakening. But this is no vain call without action. Pickowicz lays out a careful, Biblical and practical plan for spiritual renewal. His remedies are needed not only in the unique environs of the Northeast, but all across the North American continent. The Church desperately needs revival and this book lays out the prescription for it."

—SCOTT CHRISTENSEN, pastor and author of *What About Free Will?*

"Nate Pickowicz dares to dream that New England can once again be ablaze with gospel light but, more importantly, tells the church what it will cost and how it can happen. This book neither longs for the revivalistic past nor laments that a post-Christian society cannot be reached. With a call to hope and holiness, his prescription is biblical, historical, practical, and essential. This could be the spark God uses to fan into flame a different kind of revival than New England has ever seen."

—HERSHAEL W. YORK, Victor & Louise Lester Professor of Preaching, Southern Baptist Theological Seminary, Louisville, KY; Pastor, Buck Run Baptist Church, Frankfort, KY

"Is New England forsaken? Certainly not. The land of the Puritans can be revived. Nate Pickowicz beautifully shows us how."

—Todd Friel, host of Wretched Radio/TV

"In his excellent book, *Reviving New England*, Nate Pickowicz builds a case for what it will take to see New England alive with the gospel as it was in the 18th and 19th century. Do you remember the First and Second Awakening, and subsequent revivals, which gave birth to the Modern Missions Movement that has now taken the gospel to every nation of the world? One name brings this incredible history of the gospel in New England to mind like no other, the era of Jonathan Edwards. In this book, Nate envisions a pathway that would bring the gospel to every town and neighborhood through planting churches and reclaiming pulpits with the gospel and sound exegetical preaching. We need a whole new generation to be raised up, equipped, and sent into the once ripe fields of the harvest in New England. Nate shares from both an historical and personal perspective how more and more churches and pulpits in more and more towns and neighborhoods can be alive with gospel preaching, discipleship, and evangelism. This book will change your life if you are looking for a mission in New England that can impact America and the world with the truth of the gospel."

—VES SHEELY, Superintendent,
New England District Association, EFCA.

"The history of "Christian" New England can be a daunting one to catalog. Nate has given a perspective that is needed in this day and age. The future of New England lies in its revival. To be a part of that, Nate rightly states, 'We cannot be focused on self-preservation, whether it be our traditionalism or our buildings. We cannot be focused on simply meeting felt needs to no end, engaging in a social gospel. Instead, we must keep our focus on the commands of Jesus Christ, who Himself is 'the author and perfecter of faith' (Heb. 12:2). We must humbly confess that He knows what is best for the church, as the church belongs to Him. The Lord sets the agenda and commands us to follow His plan.' This book is a needful resource to that end."

—TERRY WRAGG, Pastor, Fellowship Bible Church, Chester, NH

"Those of us who have labored in New England for the glory of Christ know all too well how desperately in need the Church is for a radical work of God's Spirit to purify and revive. The church cannot afford to waste time with the world's insufficient solutions to this present darkness. *Reviving New England* is a call to pastors and churches to return to the Bible's prescription for the present darkness in which the church finds herself. Pastor Nate Pickowicz, drawing upon his own pastoral experience, has carefully and helpfully identified the most essential foundations which the church must embrace and practice if we are to experience God's restored favor. I warmly recommend this book for all who are laboring for Christ's glory in difficult places."

—JIMMY SNOWDEN, Pastor, Franklin, NH

"Every generation of Christians must affirm whether they are going to stand fast on the gospel or whether they are going to compromise. In our own day, we are seeing people abandoning biblical Christianity right and left. Instead of standing fast on and for biblical orthodoxy, many Christians focus only on their experience. This is why Nate Pickowicz wrote *Reviving New England*. This book is part church history, part examining the problems with churches in New England, and is a biblical-theological manifesto for how biblical Christianity should function. Whether you are wondering how to preach, whether church membership is biblical, or about the problems in churches in New England, reading *Reviving New England* will help you. Reading this book will help you to discover what gospel-centered, gospel-driven ministry looks like from the Word of God. Our day needs such Christians who stand not only on the Word, but also with the long line of godly saints who have gone before us. I commend *Reviving New England* to you and pray it will help you to understand the great need of the hour not only in New England but also in every community and the local church."

—DAVE JENKINS, Executive Director, Servants of Grace Ministries; Executive Editor, Theology for Life Magazine

Reviving
NEW ENGLAND

THE KEY TO REVITALIZING POST-CHRISTIAN AMERICA

NATE PICKOWICZ

ENTREATINGFAVOR.com

ISBN: 978-1539074359

First Edition

Scripture taken from the NEW AMERICAN STANDARD BIBLE®,
Copyright © 1960,1962,1963,1968,1971,1972,1973,1975,1977,
1995 by The Lockman Foundation. Used by permission.

Cover design: Stephen Melniszyn, Stephen Melniszyn Designs,
Tulsa, Oklahoma

Front cover image courtesy of Shutterstock.com
Back cover image courtesy of Marty Symons via Adobe Stock

Interior layout: John Manning

TO JESSIE

The one my soul loves

TABLE OF CONTENTS

Acknowledgments

The fact that this book made it this far is a testament to God's goodness. I love New England, and my heart's desire is that God would be glorified there again. Even if the Lord would choose to move in the heart of just one person, this project has been worth it.

I'm very grateful to several people: Dr. Steven J. Lawson, for your contagious passion, your encouragement, and for doing me the honor of writing the foreword; Scott Christensen, Terry Melle, and Jimmy Snowden, for reading the earliest drafts and giving me wise and helpful feedback; Mike Abendroth, for taking me under your wing; Dr. Hershael York, Terry Wragg, and Ves Sheely, for supporting and endorsing the project; Todd Friel and Andy Olson, for heartily promoting this book during its early stages. Without the labor of Jill Cox, Stephen Melniszyn, and John Manning, I would have been lost at each step of the process.

I continue to praise God for Harvest Bible Church—a church full of beloved saints who have treated me better than I deserve. I praise the Lord for Landon Chapman, my dear friend, along with Deering Dyer and Kofi Adu-Boahen of Entreating Favor. Thank you Dave Jenkins, for your prayers and counsel.

My heart leaps to think of the countless friends and supporters, online and offline, who have prayed for me and voiced their support for *Reviving New England*.

Most importantly, my deepest thanks goes out to my wife, Jess. Without your selflessness and support, your enthusiasm and encouragement, your patience and perseverance, this book would still be just a dream. You are God's greatest gift to me, this side of heaven.

FOREWORD

The greatest movement of the Holy Spirit upon American soil was, arguably, the first and second Great Awakenings of the eighteenth and nineteenth centuries. These seasons of revival in the churches and institutions of the early Colonies and in a newly-established nation took place in its Northeast region known as New England. It was here, where the Pilgrims and Puritans first settled, that the fire of God kindled the believers until they were ignited with fiery devotion for Jesus Christ. In the centuries since, no American revival has superseded what God did in this early stage of our history.

Since that time, the Northeast has been in steady spiritual decline. Churches, once ablaze for God, have become little more than extinguished embers amid the ashes. Pulpits, once sounding boards for the gospel, have become silent. The light of truth has been hidden under a bushel. Liberalism rules the day. False gospels abound. Dead tradition reigns. Consequently, believers are withering. Evangelism is stagnated. And congregations are shrinking. The area has become known as the graveyard of ministers.

The greatest need of the hour is for a genuine revival to strike New England again with the spiritual force of a category five hurricane. A gentle breeze will not do in such desperate days. The gale winds of heaven must blow and the churches be propelled forward in their mission. What God did in the past in the Northeast, He must do again.

The only hope for the spiritual deadness of New England is a genuine revival. A mere reorganization of the church will not suffice. Nothing short of a true awakening will suffice, one that is Scripture-expounding, God-glorifying, Christ-exalting, Spirit-empowering, heart-piercing, sin-exposing, repentance-granting, worship-revitalizing, holiness-producing, soul-converting, and world-changing. Anything less will be putting band-aids on a spiritual cancer.

Let us be encouraged. The Lord of heaven never requires the circumstances to be just right before He can do His work. It is during the darkest hours of history that He has been pleased to do His greatest work. When Satan is doing his worst, God often chooses to do His best. The clock has struck midnight in New England. A thick veil of darkness has enveloped the land. The trumpet blast of the word of God must once again awaken the slumbering congregations of this region.

This is why I am grateful that you are holding this book in your hands, *Reviving New England*, written by Nate Pickowicz. This author has done the church a great service by writing this plea that calls for another Great Awakening to come to this barren wasteland. However, this book is more than a plea. It contains a strategic plan for restoring God's work in the Northeast. You will find that this book outlines the steps to be followed for the road to recovery. This work both diagnoses the fatal disease and prescribes the strong medicine needed for the healing of our churches in this day. It is a book that needs to be injected into your spiritual bloodstream and surge through your soul.

May God use the message of this book to awaken His church in New England as He did in days of old. May a new generation of Jonathan Edwardses and George Whitefields mount its pulpits. May a new wave of David Brainerds be sent out from its prayer meetings. May a new day of spiritual power be restored to its churches as once electrified the early Colonies so long ago.

Soli Deo Gloria,
Steven J. Lawson
Dallas, Texas

Introduction

In the year we planted our church, I bumped into a traveling "revivalist" who handed me a business card and told me to call him, so that he could "bring the Spirit" to my church. He made it seem like, if I *didn't* bring him to my church, we were doomed to fail. I wondered, since the Spirit cannot be bought (Acts 8:9-24) or brought (John 1:12-13; 3:8), how could any "revivalist" guarantee revival at my church? It would seem that any genuine move of the Spirit is a supernatural work of God. What, then, does it take to bring revival to a church?

In the last few decades, we have seen a seismic shift in America, away from a Christian-sensitive culture, toward a postmodern pagan culture that is growing hostile to Christianity. While it can be argued that America was never "a Christian nation" per se, it was certainly founded by people sympathetic to Judeo-Christian values. However, the tide is turning. The days of widespread acceptance are behind us. In response to this tectonic shift, the visible church has been scrambling to do all it can to preserve its societal standing. Churches have adopted business models and practices, pastors have watered down their sermons, praise bands have taken to performing rock concerts during the worship services, the Bible and theology have been minimized, pragmatism has taken a front seat, even the gospel itself has been minimized to a dangerous level—all to attract churchgoers, thus producing numerical growth. This often gets labeled "revival." However, in many cases, these efforts consist of nothing more than man-made gimmicks that produce no lasting effects and create false converts.

We long for the days when stadiums were filled with people, listening to gospel preaching. We want to see lost sinners saved and reconciled to God through Jesus Christ. But more than anything, we desperately want to see God honored and glorified.

At one point in history, one area of the country stood as the stalwart of Christianity in America. It was a seedbed for ministry, training, and missions. It was home to the Puritans, Jonathan Edwards and the Great Awakening, Adoniram Judson and the worldwide missionary movement, and Harold Ockenga and the origins of evangelicalism. In the course of our history, no region has had more lasting impact than New England.

Over the last hundred years, however, New England has fallen into deep spiritual decline. Regular church attendance has dropped dramatically. To counter the trend, many churches have either modified their services to become more "seeker-friendly," or they have closed their doors altogether. Christian influence is nearly non-existent, and the gospel itself is all but lost.

New England was once the tip of the cultural spear, blazing a trail for the rest of the nation to follow. But now, it is dead weight, dragging down the American church. If something does not change, the Northeast will inevitably lead the rest of the nation into the depths of spiritual depression. New England is now a mission field. It is the poster child of post-Christian America. But what if genuine revival took place? If God were to ignite a fire in the Northeast, it could be the exciting force to usher in true Christian revival nationwide.

This is why I believe the key to revitalizing America is, first, to revive New England.

1

"O Lord, Give Me New England!"

As I drive past old, dilapidated church buildings, I cannot help but feel a profound sense of sadness. These proud, peeling towers serve as a grim reminder of what New England once was. It's been said that before preaching his revival sermons, Jonathan Edwards would pray, crying out, "O Lord, give me New England!" When I survey the barren spiritual wasteland of the Northeast, I find myself uttering the same plea, *"O Lord, give me New England!"*

For any Christian who lives up here, the problem is obvious. We even jokingly call ourselves "the frozen chosen"—no doubt a nod to our frigid winters, as well as our cold spiritual temperature. Yes, even our Christians are sluggish, weakened, often depressed. But driving by all of these big, white buildings—many of which have been sold and turned into libraries, karate dojos, restaurants and bars—only adds salt to the wound. It reminds us that, at one time in history, we were a shining city on a hill. And now, it's all but gone.

Prior to the Great Awakening, Jonathan Edwards would have experienced a similar sadness, as he remembered back to the spiritually rich days of the Puritans, who had bravely made their way over from England to settle in Plymouth, Massachusetts in 1620. With King James I breathing threats against them if they did not conform to the Church of England's standards, the Puritan Separatists escaped corrupted religion and profane culture to start fresh and give their children an opportunity to live out their faith unhindered.

By 1630, nearly 20,000 Puritan settlers would make their way to New England. However, these later Pilgrims were not Separatists, but Puritan Reformers. They still called the Church of England their "dear Mother"[1] but longed to reform its practices to reflect those of the New Testament churches. They were Congregationalists, devoted to the doctrines of grace, and to the Reformation. While the establishment of the Massachusetts Bay Colony served as the birthplace of the future nation, it also was the birthplace of Christianity in America. What is perhaps so shocking is the way in which the colony was established. Historian B.K. Kuiper writes,

> You would expect this Massachusetts Bay Colony with its wealth and numbers to take the lead in directing the church life and government in New England. But it was rather the little band of poor and despised radicals at Plymouth who laid the foundations of New England, and supplied the model of church government for the Bay Colony and all the New England Puritans.[2]

In the early years, the settlers of the Massachusetts Bay Colony were able to maintain the religious standards they set for themselves. They saw themselves as "a covenanted community dedicated to God's purposes."[3] In fact, they were so influential, the general standard of religious life in all subsequent colonies was known as "The New England Way." Not all of the first settlers were Puritan Christians, but the leading founders were—men like John Winthrop, John Cotton, William Bradford, and Increase and Cotton Mather. While many in the Church of England were "unfit to be members even of the visible church, persons who had never submitted voluntarily to the gospel and whose behavior advertised their indifference to God's commandments,"[4] the New England settlers were devoted to God, and free to

---

[1] B.K. Kuiper, *The Church in History*. (reprinted; Grand Rapids, MI: Eerdmans, 1996), 328.
[2] Ibid.
[3] Everett Emerson, *Puritanism in America 1620-1750*. (Boston, MA: Twayne, 1977), 92.
[4] Edmund S. Morgan, *Visible Saints: The History of the Puritan Idea*. (New York, NY: New York University Press, 1963), 33.

establish churches whose members were genuine Christian believers, saved by faith alone in Jesus Christ.

The Puritans valued good preaching, sound doctrine, holy living, and discipleship. The Church of England, even though technically "Protestant" in designation, still did not value faithfulness, righteousness, and individual soul liberty. Much of English religion was politicized. Overseas, the fires of Reformation had simmered down to lukewarm coals, and while many migrated to America in the early 1600s for various reasons, many residents writing back to England argued that "the only valid reason for migrating to Massachusetts was religion."[5] In short, the Puritans' primary focus was to establish "pure" churches. All of the best elements of the Reformation—sound doctrine, biblical preaching, church purity, education, the priesthood of all believers—were the sought-after elements. For a short season, the New England Puritans attained what they were striving for. While they failed to create "New Jerusalem" on American soil, they succeeded in creating a society that embraced Christianity.

However, zeal for religious purity eventually produced hypocritical legalism and rigid formalism. By the end of the seventeenth century, many of the institutional churches in New England had a form of godliness, yet were empty of spiritual power. Their love for God and others had grown cold, while their fear of "worldliness" soon became manic. The hysteria came to a head during the 1692-1693 Salem Witch Trials, where twenty people were executed for supposedly practicing witchcraft. While obviously a low point in the history of America, it was indicative of the spiritual temperature of the New England people. But a new day was dawning.

Jonathan Edwards and the First Great Awakening

Jonathan Edwards was born in 1703, right in the midst of spiritual decline. However, men like Edwards' grandfather, Solomon Stoddard, worked tirelessly to bring about revival in the hearts of the people.

Small town churches like Northampton revered their local pastors as leaders in the public square. Pastors had a spiritual and moral

---

[5] Emerson, *Puritanism in America*, 32.

clout that was unique among other leaders, and the people yielded their lives to their oversight. Solomon Stoddard was nicknamed "the Pope of the Connecticut Valley"[6] and had become a local legend in the frontier towns of western Massachusetts. Stoddard had "broadened the standards for full church membership to all adults who professed the doctrines of the church, submitted to its discipline, and promised to attempt to live morally."[7] Further, he kept alive the old Puritan "half-way covenant"—a concession for young children of unbelieving parents who had not yet made a profession of faith in Jesus Christ, but were granted the privilege of baptism in hopes that they would one day become true believers. Jonathan Edwards, who would take over when his grandfather died in 1729, was not as eager to make such provisions.

Instead of simply maintaining the status quo, Edwards dug in his heels, preaching and praying for genuine conversion and for godliness. He was after hearts, not memberships. Many youth in the Northampton church were engaged in sinful behavior and Edwards found himself pleading with them for their eternal salvation. He would begin preaching for spiritual revival, which would break out in December 1734. By the spring, the whole town was enraptured with nothing but spiritual things, and Edwards himself noticed a change in the attitudes and behaviors of the people. In Northampton, a town of a thousand, as many as 300 people made professions of saving faith in Jesus Christ within a six-month period![8] Such widespread revival was not limited to Northampton alone. According to Edwards himself, thirty-two communities experienced awakening during 1734-1735.[9]

The phenomenon was so unparalleled, Edwards took to writing an account of the awakenings in New England. Prominent Boston pastor Benjamin Colman sent the letter overseas to famous pastor and hymn-writer Isaac Watts in London. Eventually, a fuller draft of the

[6] Stephen J. Nichols, "Jonathan Edwards: His Life and Legacy" eds. John Piper & Justin Taylor, *A God Entranced Vision of All Things*. (Wheaton, IL: Crossway, 2004), 39.

[7] George M. Marsden, *A Short Life of Jonathan Edwards*. (Grand Rapids, MI: Eerdmans, 2008), 36.

[8] Thomas S. Kidd, *The Great Awakening: The Roots of Evangelical Christianity in Colonial America*. (New Haven, CT: Yale, 2007), 19.

[9] Ibid., 18.

letter would be published in 1737 titled, *A Faithful Narrative of the Surprising Work of God*. This exciting work, chronicling the New England awakenings, would find its way into the hands of John and Charles Wesley, as well as the famous itinerant preacher, George Whitefield.

By 1738, Whitefield was making plans to visit America to take part in God's amazing work. He was already drawing crowds by the thousands in England, and the anticipation of his arrival overseas was at a fever pitch. After visiting Savannah, Georgia in 1738, he arrived for a second time in Philadelphia in the fall of 1739. During his preaching tours up and down the eastern seaboard, Whitefield received a letter from Jonathan Edwards, eager to have him visit Northampton on his way back up. Whitefield obliged and the two met for the first time on October 17, 1740.

People flocked by the thousands to hear George Whitefield preach. It's been said that Whitefield "preached like a lion… [with] force and vehemence and passion."[10] Even as Whitefield preached at Northampton, Edwards himself sat in the front, weeping as he listened. Whitefield had a way about him by which he stirred the affections of his hearers. George Marsden notes, "Seldom did he preach a sermon in which he did not weep and reduce multitudes to tears."[11] Whitefield even joyfully lamented, "So many persons come to me under conviction and for advice, that I have scarcely time to eat bread. Wonderful things are doing here. The Word runs like lightning!"[12] And while many critics wondered about the lasting effects of his preaching, Edwards was careful to note a substantial change in the Northampton residents who had sat under Whitefield's preaching.[13] In fact, in the wake of Whitefield's departure in October 1740, Edwards would evaluate the movement, testing it against the Word of God. He would bear witness to the authenticity of the Great Awakening in his 1741 work, *The Distinguishing Marks of a Work of the Spirit of God*.

---

[10] John Gillies quoted in Steven J. Lawson, *The Evangelistic Zeal of George Whitefield*. (Orlando, FL: Reformation Trust, 2013), 100.

[11] George M. Marsden, *Jonathan Edwards: A Life*. (New Haven, CT: Yale University Press, 2003), 206.

[12] Raymond C. Ortland, Jr., *When God Comes to Church: A Biblical Model for Revival Today*. (Grand Rapids, MI: Baker Books, 2000), 40.

[13] Kidd, *The Great Awakening*, 87.

Perhaps Jonathan Edwards is best known for his landmark sermon, "Sinners in the Hands of an Angry God." On his way to Enfield, Connecticut, Edwards was traveling from Northampton to bring encouragement. Upon his arrival, however, he was met with the news that the scheduled preacher had been taken ill. Providentially, Edwards just happened to have a sermon manuscript in his saddlebag; a sermon he had preached in his own church only a few months back, though it had little impact. Over the last few years, the surrounding towns had been in the midst of an intense revival, but Enfield had yet to be moved. But, on July 8, 1741, the sermon, "Sinners in the Hands of an Angry God" was preached, and the town erupted into spiritual revival.

By Edwards' own account, he believed that the Great Awakening had reached its peak in January of 1742. Out of a population of 300,000 in New England, it's believed that between 25,000 and 50,000 new members were added to the churches at the height of the Awakening.[14] In some cases, revival preachers had pressed for revival with various tactics, taking a more radical approach. Historian Thomas Kidd notes, "By March 1743, the evangelical movement in New England and the Middle Colonies had publicly split between the radicals and moderates."[15] Generally, it has been believed that the Great Awakening ended somewhere in the mid-1740s, and in most parts of the country, it had.

While I had always believed New England's prominence in American Christianity ended with the Great Awakening, it does not seem to be the case. Even after the revival fires had died down in the larger Northeast cities, it was the frontier towns in northern New England that continued to experience revival. Starting in 1762, "a number of New England's formerly radical evangelical churches witnessed another round of awakenings."[16] This revival, known as "the Seacoast Revival," lasted until 1765. These revivals prove that the Great Awakening lasted beyond the 1740s. After 1760, the nation was undergoing a dramatic shift as religion was now beginning to play a major role in public life.[17]

---

[14] Kuiper, *The Church in History*, 345.

[15] Kidd, *The Great Awakening*, 155.

[16] Ibid., 267-268.

[17] Alister McGrath, *Christianity's Dangerous Idea: The Protestant Revolution—A History from the Sixteenth Century to the Twenty-First.* (New York, NY: HarperOne, 2007), 158.

It is also generally believed that Christianity had suffered greatly during the time of the American Revolution, thus necessitating the Second Great Awakening, but Kidd notes that there were even post-Revolutionary revivals going on in New Hampshire and Maine. He writes that "Calvinist Baptist revivals proceeded in Loudon, Barrington, Gilmanton, and Madbury."[18] S.M. Houghton cites that between 1798 and 1803, more than 150 New England churches were experiencing revival.[19] Even with the larger movement dying down and the itinerant preachers gone, the faithful pastors of the small towns of New England still stirred up their congregations through the ministry of the Word of God.

The Second Great Awakening

At the dawn of the nineteenth century, Christianity in America was waning and the world sat helplessly in the clutches of The Enlightenment—a radical movement away from faith and religion, towards science, culture, and philosophy. There were many who questioned how Christianity would fare through these years, and hope seemed dim. But a spark would be ignited in New England that would set America ablaze and shine the light of the gospel to the farthest reaches of the unknown world. This would be an age of missions, and it would all find its origin in a relatively small piece of American territory.

The event known as the Second Great Awakening was the single largest religious movement in our nation's history. Generally, it is believed to have spanned thirty years, from 1800-1830. The undisputed star of the Second Awakening was native New Englander Charles G. Finney, a high-powered evangelist who used various tactics to incite seekers into making professions of faith. He is credited with popularizing the "altar call" and the "anxious bench." While most believe Finney to have been the driving force behind the Second Great Awakening, historian Iain Murray notes that the first leaders of the movement were, in fact, faithful small-town preachers in the Northeast

---

[18] Kidd, *The Great Awakening*, 315.
[19] S.M. Houghton, *Sketches in Church History.* (Edinburgh: Banner of Truth, 1980), 210.

whose 'preaching was not in man's wisdom, but in demonstration of the Spirit and with power'—is of men whose names are unknown today. They were preachers who 'would quote chapter and verse from all parts of both Testaments, without turning over a single leaf'...[20]

Of the many New England ministers, Murray notes the dynamic ministries of Edward Dorr Griffin, Asahel Nettleton, Lyman Beecher, Edward Payson, and Gardiner Spring. In evaluating the fruit of the Second Great Awakening, he notes the superficiality of overzealous revivalist preachers' tactics versus the lasting fruit produced in the Northeast at the hands of more mature pastors—those devoted to faithful Bible preaching and teaching to nourish their churches. In fact, "revivals did not occur in conjunction with any special efforts. They were not worked up, but were witnessed in the course of the ordinary services of the churches."[21] Not only had revival fires been stirred up because of their years of faithful ministry, but the movement was also sustained through their tireless efforts. When Finney himself lamented the steady decline of revivalism on a national scale, there were many in New England towns who were still on-fire for Jesus Christ.

A Light to the Nations

While revivalism produced many flash-in-the-pan converts, it also helped create a fertile seedbed in which gospel fruit would produce a crop thirty, sixty, and a hundred fold! It was during this time—the early nineteenth century—that America would establish itself as a light to the nations, and the source of that light emanated from New England.

Earlier in 1795, Timothy Dwight—the grandson of Jonathan Edwards—became president of Yale College in Connecticut. In his early years at the school, he preached sermons and lectures on the dangers of false gospel. In the wake of his lectures, revival broke out at the school and one third of the students were converted.[22] The revival soon spread to other colleges, and by 1802, Dartmouth, Am-

[20] Iain H. Murray, *Revival and Revivalism: The Making and Marring of American Evangelicalism 1750-1858*. (Edinburgh: Banner of Truth, 1994), 193.

[21] Ibid., 208.

[22] Kuiper, *The Church in History*, 356.

herst, Williams, and the College of New Jersey were ignited by the gospel.[23] Suddenly, eager young students were being stirred up and desired to bring the good news of salvation to all nations. To meet the increased number of ministry volunteers, denominations began to form various missionary societies, publish magazines, and found Christian colleges and seminaries. In 1810, the Congregationalists formed the American Board of Commissioners for Foreign Missions, which would send 694 missionaries over the next thirty years.[24] To meet the need for Bibles and evangelistic literature, the American Bible Society (1816) and the American Tract Society (1825) were founded.

The Baptists, while dormant during the eighteenth century, erupted in the early 1800s, planting churches all through the United States, and founding Brown University (1804), which would train and send out missionaries worldwide, such as New Englanders Adoniram Judson and Luther Rice. Later, in 1889, Baptist A.J. Gordon would found the Boston Missionary Training Institute, which would eventually become Gordon College. Although not technically in New England, Princeton Theological Seminary would be founded in New Jersey (1812), and would remain a conservative stalwart for the next hundred years. There can be no question: the work done in the Northeast in the early 1800s served to expand the kingdom of God in a way not seen since the Reformation, perhaps even since the early first-century church. In 1831, French philosopher Alexis de Tocqueville remarked, "There is no country in the world where the Christian religion retains a greater influence over the souls of men than in America."[25]

Decline in the Northeast

For nearly three hundred years, New England had been a beacon of light to the nations. From the earliest days of the Puritanical devotion of the first settlers, to the heartfelt revival preaching of the Great Awakening, to the evangelistic and missionary zeal of nineteenth cen-

---

[23] Ibid.
[24] Ibid., 359.
[25] Murray, *Revival and Revivalism*, 117.

tury believers, the Northeast had manifested a consistent witness to the whole world. But by the early twentieth century, New England began to grow cold.

Today, the current landscape is but a shadow of the glory it once was. Like the apostate people of ancient Israel before the captivity, the people of New England have gone wayward and no longer call on the Lord their God. How did this happen? There are at least four factors that have contributed to the downfall of biblical Christianity in New England.

First, *the introduction of liberalism into colleges and universities.* As early as the 1700s, Rationalism and Deism had swept across the Atlantic from Europe and embedded itself into the institutions of higher learning. Only sixteen years after the Plymouth landing, Harvard College was founded for the purpose of training "the English and Indian youth in knowledge and godliness,"[26] but by 1700, the school had grown cold under the chill of liberalism. By the early 1800s, men like Yale's president Nathaniel Taylor "knew that modern liberal Christianity, especially Unitarianism, was changing the face of Christian education in New England,"[27] and vowed to rescue the schools. But all of the Ivy League giants—Harvard, Yale, Dartmouth, Brown, and Princeton—would eventually cave to liberalism, and culture quickly followed.

Second, *the propagation of Unitarianism and Universalism.* It wouldn't be long before the heresies being taught in the colleges and seminaries would make their way into the churches. Along with the rejection of Christian orthodoxy with regards to the Trinity, Unitarianism is built on Rationalism, stressing individualism and freedom of the human will. This idea became popular in mostly Anglican and Congregationalist circles in the Northeast.[28] Made popular by the Methodists, such as John Murray (1741-1785), Universalism—the doctrine that all people will be saved regardless of their belief—made its way into New England as well.

---

[26] Houghton, *Sketches in Church History*, 172.

[27] Douglas A. Sweeney and Allen C. Guelzo, eds. *The New England Theology: From Jonathan Edwards to Edwards Amasa Park.* (Grand Rapids, MI: Baker, 2006), 187.

[28] Justo L. Gonzales, *The Story of Christianity Volume II: The Reformation to the Present Day.* (New York, NY: HarperOne, 2010), 320.

Both of these doctrines were a denial of orthodoxy and severely crippled the once-faithful mainline denominations.

Third, *prosperity mixed with self-reliance.* While the Boston economy had been booming since its beginning, the overall wealth of Americans in the late 1800s was increasing. The publishing of Ralph Waldo Emerson's essay, "Self-Reliance" (1841), classified a whole generation of people who were being steered away from religion—trusting in God—to trusting in their own ability to earn wealth and succeed. This vein of staunch individualism has been carved in the stone granite hearts of New Englanders.

Last, *the gutting of the gospel and biblical preaching from pulpits.* As we will see, the gospel is the foundation of Christianity and the only means by which people can be saved, and the advent of liberal doctrines completely removed the preaching of the biblical gospel from many New England pulpits. Further, preachers began to move away from the faithful exposition of Bible texts—a nonnegotiable practice of the Puritans, as well as Edwards and Whitefield, but absent in later generations.

There can be no doubt that the theological perversion of biblical doctrine, the introduction of liberalism, sinful individualism, and the jettisoning of the gospel, all had a hand in plunging the region of New England into its present spiritual darkness.

Surveying the Landscape

At this point, we know that, spiritually speaking, things in New England are bad, but the question is: How bad is it? One way to answer this is to examine the influence of Christianity in New England. This is a more challenging undertaking than one might think. According to Pew Research Center, 65% of residents in the Northeast identify as "Christian."[29] But is it true that more than 6 out of 10 New Englanders are saved and headed for heaven? Well, naturally, we must then examine: What does it mean to be a "Christian"?

---

[29] http://www.pewforum.org/religious-landscape-study/region/northeast/ (accessed August 29, 2015).

In his book *The Great Evangelical Recession*, John Dickerson assesses what it means to be a "Christian" in America. Laying aside the existence of cultural Christianity, he writes, "We're talking about American Christians who believe the Bible is God's Word, that it is without error, and that Jesus is the only way to salvation and to God."[30] In other words, we mean those who believe the gospel as revealed in the Scriptures. Albert Mohler explains that there are doctrines that are "most central and essential to the Christian faith... such as the Trinity, the full deity and humanity of Jesus Christ, justification by faith, and the authority of Scripture."[31] These are the gospel essentials; the fundamentals of Christianity that cannot be compromised. To deny these truths, whether corporately or individually, is to deny Christianity.

If we are to determine a "Christian" by an orthodox view of salvation and the Bible, then the picture changes drastically. Examining national trends, Dickerson cites four comprehensive studies and concludes: "At best, according to the most optimistic reports, we are two in ten Americans... [but] by multiple accounts, evangelical believers are between 7 and 9 percent of the United States population."[32] He astutely notes that while "a lot of Americans *say* they're born again, when prodded, they do not believe what evangelical Christians believe."[33] If Dickerson's research is correct, and the national Christian population is less than 10 percent, then how much smaller is Christian population in the Northeast?

When we re-examine the Pew Research Center's data in light of Dickerson's findings, we quickly note that of the 65% of Northeast "Christians," 30% identify as Catholic, and 15% identify as Mainline Protestant. While some would balk at the idea of calling adherents to these groups *non-Christian*, it must be recognized that, generally, these two groups deny many of the tenets of the gospel and Scriptural authority. It has been witnessed over and over again that people in these two groups, while claiming to be "Christian," do not consistently demon-

---

[30] John S. Dickerson, *The Great Evangelical Recession*. (Grand Rapids, MI: Baker-Books, 2013), 24.
[31] R. Albert Mohler, Jr. *The Disappearance of God: Dangerous Beliefs in the New Spiritual Openness*. (Colorado Springs, CO: Multnomah, 2009), 3.
[32] Dickerson, *The Great Evangelical Recession*, 26.
[33] Ibid., 28. Italics original.

strate that they hold to a biblical worldview, and certainly not an understanding of the salvation as spelled out in the Bible.[34] When we examine the numbers of those who belong to Bible-believing, gospel-preaching churches, the numbers drop dramatically.

In her article, "Re-evangelizing New England," Ruth Graham notes that "less than 3 percent of the region's population is evangelical Christians."[35] Missiologist J.D. Payne has surveyed individual cities and found New England cities to be the least in total evangelical percentage—Pittsfield, MA (1.5%), Barnstable-Yarmouth, MA (1.5%), Providence, RI (1.7%), Boston, MA (2.5%), Hartford, CT (2.7%), Burlington, VT (2.9%), and Bangor, ME (3.8%).[36] These and other factors have caused many to consider New England an "unreached people group."

It must be said that merely *belonging* to an Evangelical denomination means nothing. Certainly there are unsaved people in Bible-teaching churches. Conversely, there may be genuine believers in non-gospel churches. Faith must be measured individually, not corporately, and only God truly knows the heart. But even if we are optimistic, the number of Christian believers does not seem much higher than 2 or 3 percent. Further, to test this theory, even if we were to ignore the statistics for a minute, this fact would become evident if we added up the average attendance of Bible churches in our neighborhoods and compared those numbers to the total population. The picture is very grim; we are a region full of lost people.

What we need is revival.

What is Revival?

The term "revival" did not come into common English usage until the time of Cotton Mather (1663-1728).[37] It must be noted that *revival* is

---

[34] Rom. 3:28; 1 Cor. 15:3-4; Gal. 2:16; Eph. 2:8-9.

[35] http://www.slate.com/articles/life/faithbased/2012/11/re_evangelizing_new_england_how_church_planting_and_music_festivals_are.html (accessed December 20, 2015).

[36] http://www.jdpayne.org/2010/06/02/least-evangelical-u-s-metro-areas/ (accessed August 29, 2015).

[37] Iain H. Murray, *Pentecost-Today? The Biblical Basis for Understanding Revival.* (Edinburgh: Banner of Truth, 1998), 3.

different than *revivalism*—the former being historically understood as "a surprising work of God" versus the latter, a man-made movement propagated to guarantee conversion results.[38] It must be understood that "evangelical Christians are all agreed that [revival] has to do with the person and work of the Holy Spirit."[39] According to J.I. Packer, "Revival is God touching minds and hearts in an arresting, devastating, exalting way, to draw them to himself through working from the inside out rather than from the outside in."[40] Restated and expanded by Iain Murray,

> a revival is an outpouring of the Holy Spirit, brought about by the intercession of Christ, resulting in a new degree of life in the churches and a widespread movement of grace among the unconverted. It is an extraordinary communication of the Spirit of God, a superabundance of the Spirit's operations, and enlargement of his manifest power.[41]

What Will Revival Produce?

While the discussion of "revival" is certainly exciting, we would do well to identify the markers of true revival. When we stop and ponder what genuine revival in New England might look like, the following markers may very well be seen.

An Increased Number of Conversions

When the gospel is preached and the Holy Spirit is moving to regenerate hearts, people believe and are saved. No one can be saved apart from the ministry of the Holy Spirit, but He will not regenerate a person without belief in the gospel (Rom. 10:14, 17; Eph. 1:13). The work of the Spirit and the gospel go hand-in-hand. In the throes of revival, a vast number of people will be responding to the gospel of Jesus Christ, and the Lord will add to the church those who are being saved.

---

[38] Murray, *Revival & Revivalism*, xviii.

[39] Murray, *Pentecost-Today?*, 4.

[40] J.I. Packer, "The Glory of God and the Reviving of Religion: A Study in the Mind of Jonathan Edwards" eds. John Piper & Justin Taylor, *A God Entranced Vision of All Things: The Legacy of Jonathan Edwards*. (Wheaton, IL: Crossway, 2004), 100.

[41] Murray, *Pentecost-Today?*, 23-24.

A Regathering and Strengthening of Back-Slidden Believers

As the Lord moves within people, He draws them to Himself (John 6:44). While many in New England have been wounded by churches in the past, a revival of God's Spirit would produce a stirring in their hearts whereby they would begin to seek the things of God again. They would return to churches. They would dust off their Bibles and study. They would shun sinful living. They would desire intimacy with God, devoting themselves to fervent prayer.

A Deepening of Devotion by Faithful Believers

The most faithful of believers would increase in faithfulness (1 Thes. 4:10-12). While they may already be pillars of godly virtue, they would continue to add to their faith and abound with a deeper love for God, for His Word, and for others. Revival would set the church on fire and they would rededicate themselves to the Great Commission.

The Strategic Value of New England

Few geographic regions have been blessed both by rich history and present influence. While New England not only holds the sweet memory of America's past, it also holds our future. Steven Lawson has said:

> In the corridors of this northeast corner of the United States, there is a vast, highly-dense population that encompasses a major portion of this country. To penetrate [New England] with the gospel is to capture a significantly large populace. The influence of this area in terms of finance, commerce, banking, media, education, politics, athletics, and the arts is, virtually, unparalleled. To reach [New England] for Christ is to exert a profound influence that reaches far beyond its borders that will impact the rest of America and, ultimately, the world. For these reasons and more, biblical preaching is desperately needed in [New England]. Given the dire state of this spiritually barren region, recapturing its pulpit must be a chief priority in this day.[42]

---

[42] http://www.necep.org/site/cpage.asp?cpage_id=140036909&sec_id=140000662 (accessed on December 20, 2015).

The need is great, the time is now. While the task seems insurmountable, the statistics are grim, and the current landscape is depressing, there has never been a more crucial time to act. Most New Englanders have never heard the gospel. Of those who are saved, many of them have not sat under sound Bible teaching, perhaps since they were children. And even many still have never known the joy that comes with deepening their love for God through Jesus Christ.

And while it must be said that true revival is "a surprising work of God," we also know that He works through the faithfulness and obedience of Christians. So, the question now is: How do we revive New England?

It starts by giving God His pulpits back.

2

Giving God His Pulpits Back

*"Preach the word; be ready in season and out of season;
reprove, rebuke, exhort, with great patience and instruction."*
2 Timothy 4:2, NASB

New England pulpits have been hijacked! They were once filled with the preaching of the Word of God, but now they are filled with the shifting opinions of sinful men. This is a tragic thing! Steven Lawson has said, "If we lose the pulpit, we lose the church; and if we lose the church, we lose the world."[1] It is from the pulpit that God speaks to His people through His word, so when His voice is removed and replaced with another, the church is quickly led astray. History bears witness to the fact that when the church loses her influence, the culture suffers, degrades, and eventually falls. But worse than the damage to culture is the absolute tragic end of souls who meet their demise without ever being reconciled to God through the gospel of Jesus Christ. I fear the souls of New Englanders are freefalling into hell, and we can no longer afford to be unaware, unaffected, and uncommitted to doing anything about it. Woe to us, if we ever concede defeat! The church must be willing to herald God's word unashamed, and in order to do this, we must be willing to give God His pulpits back.

There are Christians in New England who mourn our spiritual condition. So few believers, so many lost people. And our churches have tried every possible program and tactic to re-germinate the dead soil, but to no avail. It's no mystery that what is needed is a miracu-

---

[1] Steven J. Lawson, "Mechanics of Expository Preaching" conference session, The New England Center for Expository Preaching, Hampstead, NH (April 23, 2013).

lous work of God to regenerate and revive dead hearts. But what will bring about this work? What are the key elements essential to true revival? A brief glimpse at historical revivals may prove helpful.

Revivals in History

While there have no doubt been countless periods of spiritual revival throughout history,[2] there seems to be a common factor implicit in all of them—the proclamation of God's word. Here are a few examples:

Josiah's Reforms

In the days of apostate Israel, the young king Josiah stumbled across "the book of the law" hidden within the temple. He read it, fell under conviction by it, and ordered it to be taught to the people (2 Kings 22:8-13). Subsequently, he would institute sweeping reforms that would shape the cultural and spiritual landscape of the southern kingdom of Judah for the next hundred years.

The Ezra-Nehemiah Revival

Following their return from the Babylonian captivity, the people of Israel were in national and spiritual devastation. It would be through Nehemiah's leadership that the protective wall around Jerusalem would be rebuilt. In the wake of the completion of the wall, the people approached Ezra the priest, asking him to read aloud the law of God and explain it to them (Nehemiah 8:1-8). Upon hearing it taught, they immediately came under conviction, tearfully confessed their sin, and set their hearts to obey the Lord. This singular event marked a turning point in the life of Israel that would signify them as "the people of the book" until the days of Jesus.

The Birth of the Church

At Pentecost, the Holy Spirit descended on and indwelled Christian believers for the first time, but it was the powerful, Spirit-filled preaching of the apostle Peter that "pierced [the people] to the heart" and ushered in conversion of three thousand souls (Acts

---

[2] Walter C. Kaiser Jr. explores sixteen distinct occurrences of revival from Scripture, drawing principles for today, in *Revive Us Again: Biblical Principles for Revival Today.* Fearn, Scotland: Christian Focus, 2001.

2:14-41). This marked the beginning of the church, which has continued victoriously for more than twenty centuries (Matt. 16:18).

The Protestant Reformation

Martin Luther is often credited with igniting the Protestant Reformation when he tacked his *95 Theses* to the front door of the church in Wittenberg on October 31, 1517, but some believe that it was the publishing of Desiderius Erasmus' Greek New Testament the previous year[3] that laid the kindling wood for the spiritual fire. Once the New Testament was published in its original language, translations into the common languages of the people could be made, and once the Scriptures could be understood in a common tongue, the Word of God could be faithfully preached by such men as Martin Luther, John Calvin, and John Knox. The tremors from the Reformation are still being felt today.

The Great Awakening

As we have already seen, the Great Awakening began in New England around 1735 and lasted until roughly 1742. Generally, it was believed to have been a backlash against leniency in the church over sin. While many factors played into this seismic cultural shift, the preaching ministries of men like Jonathan Edwards and George Whitefield are credited for bringing about the greatest revival on American soil.

What do all of these revivals and more have in common? In all cases of spiritual reform and revival, it is the faithful dispensing of the Word of God that has transformed hearts and minds. However, no single method of dispensation has had a greater impact than that of faithful preaching. D. Martyn Lloyd-Jones writes,

> What is it that always heralds the dawn of a Reformation or of a Revival? It is renewed preaching. Not only a new interest in preaching but a new kind of preaching. A revival of true preaching has always heralded these great movements in the history of the Church. And, of course, when the Reformation and the Revival come they have always led

---

[3] Alister McGrath, *Christianity's Dangerous Idea.* (New York, NY: HarperOne, 2007), 36.

to great and notable periods of the greatest preaching that the Church has ever known.[4]

The question now is: Are New England pastors and preachers faithfully preaching the Word of God? By and large, I would argue that we are not.

The Sad State of New England Preaching

While it is difficult to make sweeping statements and generalizations about the preaching in the Northeast, certainly there are practices that are commonplace in our pulpits. The thrust of my concern with New England preaching is the pervasiveness of weightless sermons devoid of biblical truth. The problem is that New Englanders are consistently fed a steady diet of junk food, which leaves their souls emaciated. Speaking more broadly, Steven Lawson aptly characterizes such preaching:

> What passes for preaching in many of today's pulpits is little more than sermonettes for Christianettes. No doubt you know exactly the kind of preaching to which I am referring—20-minute pep talks filled with shallow clichés, self-help snippets, and bumper-sticker slogans.[5]

Sadly, you could stamp "New England preaching" on Lawson's description. But, for the sake of aiding in the specifics, I will address some of the individual problems in our preaching. While not an exhaustive list, here are some of the things we see:

The Topical Sermon

Topical preaching addresses a specific subject or topic, rather than a Bible text. It must be said that there is nothing inherently wrong with topical preaching that is done exegetically, that is, derived from the Bible. While topical preaching—done correctly—has its place in the pulpit ministry, a long exposure to it will tend to leave a congregation ignorant of the broader biblical narrative, and focused solely on stray doctrines or topics as if they were floating aimlessly around the room. In the end, an overexposure to topical preaching starves Christians of true biblical nourishment and stunts their spiritual growth, but it also lends itself to another problem.

---

[4] D. Martyn Lloyd-Jones, *Preaching & Preachers*. (Grand Rapids, MI: Zondervan, 1971), 24-25.
[5] Steven J. Lawson, *The Kind of Preaching God Blesses*. (Eugene, OR: Harvest House, 2013), 35.

The Hobby-Horsed Sermon

The natural result of a topical-focused preaching ministry is the bent of the preacher to hobby-horse his own preferences. While no preacher can claim to be truly impartial, the tendency of topical preachers is to select subject matter that is near and dear to their own heart. This seems harmless at first glance, but the real danger is twofold. First, the preacher may very well be presenting the congregation with a lopsided view of topics as they appear in Scripture. For example, pastors who are keen to preach on spiritual warfare tend to maximize Satan's presence and influence, to the point where he appears to be lurking around every corner. But this produces an unbalanced approach to the Bible, as Satan is a surprisingly minor figure when compared to the vast warnings against a person's own indwelling sin. The second danger is excluding doctrine from the preaching. Preachers who hand-pick their favorite topics will naturally tend to focus less on difficult subject matter such as judgment, hell, the law, election, homosexuality, divorce, spiritual gifts, and other challenging or controversial parts of Scripture.

The Newspaper Sermon

This could also be called the "what I saw on TV the other day" sermon. Generally, the preacher is grabbed by some random thought or tidbit and will decide to build a sermon around it. Certainly, there is room for spontaneity and flexibility in preaching, but as a regular practice, this leaves a congregation untethered to the Word of God, and sends them looking for prophetic meaning in every news headline. These kinds of sermons reflect a lack of discipline in preparation, as well as a lack of intentionality in caring for the flock of God.

The Political Sermon

Much like "The Newspaper Sermon" these sermons tend to reflect the political preferences of the preacher. To be clear, providing biblical teaching on pertinent issues like abortion and homosexuality is necessary in our time, but this politicized trend often reflects the pastor's own views on matters and the sermon is basically his platform for trying to get the church to vote his way. The real danger with this is that believers' identity gets built on a specific political party, leader, or cause, and not on Jesus Christ. Surely, this sort of abuse of the pulpit is terrible error.

The New Age Sermon

In the broadest terms, New Age philosophy is the religion of vague spirituality—mysticism, astrology, metaphysics, ecology, etc. Historically speaking, it's nothing more than a rebirth of second-century Gnosticism.[6] Most conservative churches do not have New Age philosophies taught from their pulpits. We've seen this come more from liberal churches and mainline denominations. But with the conservative, evangelical population as small as it is in New England, it's safe to say that there are many churches who engage in this kind of false teaching.

The Feel-Good Sermon

While the Bible includes joyful and encouraging passages (e.g. Ps. 150, Phil. 4:4, 1 Thes. 5:16-18), the goal of preaching is not simply to make people feel good, but to reveal the will of God—"for this is the will of God, your sanctification" (1 Thess. 4:3). Restated, the goal of all preaching is to be the primary vehicle by which God sanctifies His church, conforming them into the image of Christ unto His own glory. With that being said, the natural outcome of such preaching is not to produce happiness, but holiness. Feel-good preaching tends to ignore more difficult truths like sin, judgment and repentance, and replace them with spiritual anesthetic. If the preacher fails to warn his listeners of their peril and God's righteous requirement, in favor of trying to make them "feel good," he has abdicated his responsibility in ministry.

The Moralistic Sermon

While it is good to preach biblical morality in your sermon, it is dangerous to preach morality divorced from the gospel. Preaching gospel-less morality is nothing more than behavioral suggestions without the weight of biblical authority behind it. Furthermore, to instruct people to "do good things" as a means of earning favor with God is

---

[6] See the arguments made in Peter Jones, *The Gnostic Empire Strikes Back: An Old Heresy for the New Age*. Phillipsburg, NJ: Presbyterian & Reformed, 1992.

heresy; it's a false gospel of works-based salvation. The true gospel centers on the perfect morality of Christ and His satisfying the wrath of God through His substitutionary, propitiatory death on the cross. To preach good deeds only undermines the gospel, as it ignores the righteous requirements of a holy God, diminishes the sinfulness of human beings, and side-steps completely the need for Jesus Christ to come and die in the place of sinners. Beyond being anti-gospel, it actually creates an alternate religion known as Christian Moralistic Therapeutic Deism—a term coined by Christian Smith—by which adherents believe that they are "able to earn favor with God and justify [themselves] before God by virtue of [their] behavior."[7] However, the Bible asserts that this is impossible (Eph. 2:8-9; cf. Rom. 3:28; Gal. 2:16).

The Springboard Sermon

This kind of preaching often has the veneer of seeming biblical, but in actuality, it is not. Typically, a "springboard" sermon starts off with a given text, and may include a few general comments about it, but then the preacher takes off in a completely different direction, often never returning to the original text. Not only does this give no textual understanding to the listeners, but worse, it gives the impression that the preacher's personal opinions and subsequent rabbit trail is based on and supported by the given text. Whether intentional or not, this misleads the congregation. While many New England pastors might think they're being faithful because they use the Bible in their sermons, it must be said that preaching *from* the Word is very different than *preaching* the Word itself.

The Spiritualized Sermon

It is possible to select a Bible text, read it in its entirety from the pulpit, even give some facts, and yet still fail to discharge your responsibility as a preacher of the Word of God. In 2 Timothy 2:15, the apostle Paul exhorts his young disciple to "be diligent to present yourself approved to God as a workman who does not need to be ashamed, accurately handling the word of truth." This is a call for hard work, faithful study, and proper hermeneutics. Every

---

[7] Matt Chandler with Jared Wilson, *The Explicit Gospel.* (Wheaton, IL: Crossway, 2012), 13.

student of Scripture engages in hermeneutics—the art and science of interpreting the Bible. Passages of text must be interpreted in their right context and applied correctly to the modern-day believer. Many Bible texts have been wrenched out of their context and butchered through spiritualizing their meaning. Making the text mean something it was never intended to mean is called *eisegesis*, which betrays the text, rendering a sermon "unbiblical."

The Gospel-Less Sermon

The debate persists as to whether or not every sermon must contain a full gospel presentation, and whether or not every Bible text must therefore be about Jesus Christ. But the issue is not whether the full gospel needs to be in *every* sermon or not, but rather, the concern that the gospel is *never* presented in *any* sermon! And while every Bible text can be explained in light of the overarching narrative leading to Christ, certainly Jesus is not the immediate focus of every single text. To be clear, the worst thing we can do is present an audience with Bible stories and verses, yet fail to point to the cross. As Charles Spurgeon has famously said,

> The motto of all true servants of God must be, 'We preach Christ; and him crucified.' A sermon without Christ in it is like a loaf of bread without any flour in it. No Christ in your sermon, sir? Then go home, and never preach again until you have something worth preaching.[8]

So, if all these approaches and more are examples of poor preaching, then what is to be our method? What is true, God-honoring, Christ-exalting, Spirit-empowered preaching that will surely be used to set the church ablaze and revive our barren New England wasteland?

Characteristics of Faithful Preaching

Through the years, much ink has been spilled on the topic of preaching. Better men have written better books on preaching than I will ever

---

[8] Preached on July 9, 1876; sermon #2899. Quoted in https://blogs.thegospelcoalition.org/justintaylor/2010/08/04/preach-christ-or-go-home%E2%80%94and-other-classic-spurgeon-quotes-on-christless-preaching/ (accessed September 10, 2016).

hope to write, and every one of them contains various elements and marks of good preaching. It is not my goal to exhaust this topic or to explore every element, but instead, to note three main characteristics that must exist in faithful preaching. If I may, let me submit to you that in order to be found faithful, you must:

Preach Biblically

When Paul told Timothy to "preach the word" (2 Tim. 4:2), he did not mean that he was to make cursory references to obscure verses in his preaching, but rather, to make the Scriptures the *source* and the *focus* of his preaching. In other words, the content and main point of our preaching must be the self-revelation of the Person of God; in other words, the Bible. Otherwise, it cannot be called "biblical." But before we delve into what it means to "preach biblically," we must start by looking at the Bible itself.

We must affirm that the full revelation of the sixty-six books of the Bible is *inspired*; breathed-out by God (2 Tim. 3:16; 2 Pet. 1:21), *inerrant*; without error or fault in all its original content (Ps. 12:6; Matt. 5:18), *infallible*; truthful in all it claims (Rom. 3:4; Titus 1:2; Heb. 6:18), *trustworthy*; unbroken and reliable (John 10:35; Titus 1:9), *authoritative*; bearing the weight of God's own authority (Ps. 119:89; 1 Thess. 2:13), *righteous*; morally correct (Rom. 7:12; 1 Tim. 1:8), *holy*; perfectly pure and set apart from all other writing (Rom. 7:12), *living* and *active* (Hebrews 4:12), *powerful* (Heb. 4:12; Eph. 6:17), *life-giving* (Deut. 8:3; Matt. 4:4), and *sufficient*; more than enough for life and practice (Ps. 19:7-9).

If we fail to acknowledge the Bible as the perfect self-revelation of God, then we fail to fully apprehend the true character of God (John 1:1-3; cf. Ps. 33:6). Therefore, we must see that God cannot be separated from His Word,[9] and to side-step God's Word—intentionally or unintentionally—is to manifest a low view of Scripture, and subsequently, a low view of God Himself. Stated plainly: when Scripture speaks, God speaks. By faithfully declaring the truth of Scripture, the preacher is speaking on behalf of God to His people. As Steven Lawson rightly

---

[9] J.I. Packer, *"Fundamentalism" and the Word of God.* (Grand Rapids, MI: Eerdmans, 1958), 85-91. Packer astutely demonstrates the interchangeability of God and His Word, noting: "(the New Testament writers') habitual appeal to the Old Testament text

notes, "Preaching is to be the profound proclamation of the eternal message which comes from God Himself."[10]

The Word as the Source

So, what does *biblical preaching* mean? It means the Bible is your primary, secondary, and tertiary source. It means that the main idea of your sermon is not based on a TV show you recently watched, or a chapter of a book you just read. It means that you are endeavoring to deliver to God's people something *from His word*. The Bible is your main text—the authoritative source of your sermon. Bryan Chapell is correct when he says, "Without the authority of the Word, preaching becomes an endless search for topics, therapies, and techniques that will win approval, promote acceptance, advance a cause, or soothe worry."[11]

Further, your supporting texts are also from the Scriptures. The best way to interpret the Bible is not by bringing in some other authority. To do so would be an attempt to undermine the Bible's inherent authority. For example, we cannot in good conscience apply the theory of evolution to interpret Genesis, nor can we apply the methods used in secular psychology to understand the human condition. We must understand and interpret Scripture with Scripture. This is called *synthesis*.

When we employ the method of synthesis—Scripture interpreting Scripture—we are also able to derive biblical doctrine. A simple definition of doctrine would be, "What the whole Bible teaches us today about some particular topic."[12] We do not derive Christian doctrine—our theology—from religious tradition, but from carefully-interpreted, rightly-synthesized verses of Holy Scripture.

---

as to God Himself speaking, while, together, they make an irresistible impression of the absolute identification by their writers of the Scriptures in their hands with the living voice of God… God and the Scriptures are brought into such conjunction as to show that in point of directness of authority no distinction was made between them." (86)

[10] Steven J. Lawson, *Famine in the Land*. (Chicago, IL: Moody Press, 2003), 66.

[11] Bryan Chapell, *Christ-Centered Preaching*. (Grand Rapids, MI: Baker, 1994), 32.

[12] Wayne Grudem, *Systematic Theology: An Introduction to Bible Doctrine*. (Grand Rapids, MI: Zondervan, 1994), 25.

The Word of Christ as the Focus

In order to preach biblically, we must see that the Bible is not just the source of our material, but also the focus of our endeavors. It must be said that our ultimate goal is to understand God through His Son Jesus Christ. While there is no life in the literal text of the Bible, Jesus made it clear "[the Scriptures] bear witness about Me" (John 5:39). In the end, we're seeking to know and be saved by Jesus Christ.

The ultimate goal of biblical preaching is to drive believers back into the Word of God, which cleanses and nourishes them (Eph. 5:26-30). Jesus prayed to the Father to "sanctify them by the truth; Your word is truth" (John 17:17). Some have earnestly cautioned against exalting the Bible over the person of Jesus, but it's very telling that we don't see this concern from Jesus Himself (Matt. 4:4; 5:17-18; Luke 24:25-27; John 3:34; 5:39-40; 6:68). And while some would make the foolish claim that Bible-soaked believers are *bibliolaters*—idolatrous worshipers of the Bible—we must be sure to hold Scripture in the same regard that Jesus Christ did. J.I. Packer argues,

> A Christ who permits His followers to set Him up as the Judge of Scripture, One by whom its authority must be confirmed before it becomes binding and by whose adverse sentence it is in places annulled, is a Christ of human imagination, made in the theologian's own image, One whose attitude to Scripture is the opposite of that of the Christ of history. If the construction of such a Christ is not a breach of the second commandment, it is hard to see what is. It is sometimes said that to treat the Bible as the infallible word of God is idolatry. If Christ was an idolater, and if following His teaching is idolatry, the accusation may stand; not, however, otherwise. But to worship a Christ who did not receive the Scripture as God's unerring word, nor require His followers to do so, would seem to be idolatry in the strictest sense.[13]

Understanding the Scriptures is the key to understanding God, because in them, we see the revelation of Jesus Christ, who is Himself

---

[13] Packer, *Fundamentalism and the Word of God*, 61-62.

"the image of the invisible God" (Col. 1:15) and "the exact imprint of His nature" (Heb. 1:3). Charles Spurgeon is often credited with saying, "A Bible that's falling apart usually belongs to someone who isn't." The way to ignite the church is to give them the unadulterated Word of God, because in His Word, we encounter the words and works of Jesus Christ. Therefore, the Bible must be preached from our pulpits. As John MacArthur writes, "If there is to be a reformation of the pulpit, and a revival again in the church, it will only come about through God-glorifying, Christ-centered, Spirit-empowered preaching. This and this alone is the kind of preaching God blesses—biblical preaching."[14]

Preach Expositionally

The term "expositional" or "expository" preaching has gotten a bad rap through the years. Often times, it is assumed that expository preaching means dry ninety-minute sermons, or laboring in a single book of the Bible for decades, or droning on with word studies and Greek tenses, etc. But these are merely gross characterizations, and do not really reflect the true heart of expository preaching.

At its most basic level, *expository* preaching is that which starts from the biblical text and "exposes" its full meaning to the hearers. In fact, you might even call it "exploratory" preaching, as the preacher is endeavoring to plumb the depths of a given verse or passage, unwilling to relent until a satisfactory understanding is attained. In their helpful book, *Preach*, Mark Dever and Greg Gilbert define it this way: "*Expositional preaching is preaching in which the main point of the biblical text being considered becomes the main point of the sermon being preached.*"[15] Or, as J.I. Packer writes, it is simply "letting texts talk."[16] By committing to exposition, the preacher is deferring to God's perfect judgment, allowing Him to speak to His own people. On this point, Bryan Chapell writes,

> The expository preacher opens the Bible before God's people and dares to say, 'I will explain to you what this passage means.' The words are not meant to convey one's own

---

[14] John MacArthur, from the forward of Lawson, *The Kind of Preaching God Blesses*, 9.
[15] Mark Dever and Greg Gilbert, *Preach: Theology Meets Practice.* (Nashville, TN: B&H, 2012), 36. Italics original.
[16] Quoted in Lawson, *Famine in the Land*, 19.

authority but rather humbly confess that the preacher has no better word than God's word. Thus, the preacher's mission and calling is to explain to God's people what the Bible means.[17]

Expository preaching is an exercise in constantly asking God, "What do You want to say to Your people?" It's an exploration into the very mind of God. Faithful exposition humbly unleashes a barrage of questions and seeks answers from the Scripture. It is a relentless search for the divine truth contained in the inspired text. As John Stott so eloquently writes, "The expositor pries open what appears closed, makes plain what is obscure, unravels what is knotted and unfolds what is tightly packed."[18]

But do we see a mandate for this kind of preaching in the Bible?

Nehemiah 8:7-8

Hundreds of years before the inauguration of the church, we see a typical model of preachers exhorting believers with the Word of God. At the start of the post-exilic revivals, we read: "[Ezra and the priests] explained the law to the people while the people remained in their place. And they read from the law of God, translating to give the sense so that they understood the reading." We see several key components, such as the reading of God's Word followed by clear explanation, all for the purpose of God's people coming to a clear understanding. This is Old Testament expository preaching.

Acts 8:30-31

What many would consider to be a chance encounter proved astoundingly providential as Philip the evangelist crossed paths with an Ethiopian eunuch who was perched on the back of a chariot with a copy of the prophecy of Isaiah in his lap. When Philip catches up to the chariot, he hears the Ethiopian official reading from Isaiah 53 and asks, "Do you understand what you are reading?" He replies, "Well, how could I, unless someone guides me?" Philip gladly hops up onto the chariot next to the Ethiopian official and begins to exposit the text—"And Philip opened his mouth, and

[17] Chapell, *Christ-Centered Preaching*, 30.
[18] John Stott, *Between Two Worlds: The Challenge of Preaching Today.* (Grand Rapids, MI: Eerdmans, 1982), 126.

beginning from this Scripture he preached Jesus to him" (v. 35, italics mine). While much of Scripture can be understood even by the humblest child, there is much that needs to be explained by able teachers; gifts of God to the church (Eph. 4:11).

1 Timothy 4:13

In his letter to Timothy, the apostle Paul gives specific instruction to the young pastor with regards to the ministry of the word. He tells him, "Until I come, give attention to the public reading of Scripture, to exhortation and teaching." Inherent in this verse, we see a threefold imperative for expository preaching. Re-stated principally: a) read the biblical text; b) teach the biblical text; c) exhort with the biblical text. In basic hermeneutical principles, the minister is to deal with three main questions: a) What does it say? b) What does it mean? c) How is it to be applied? One does not have to push too hard to derive our marching orders from verses like this one.

Matthew 28:19-20

Perhaps the capstone command for an expository preaching/teaching ministry comes to us in the Great Commission. After claiming full authority, Jesus delegates that authority to the disciples in order that they might further His ministry. He tells them, "Go therefore and *make disciples* of all the nations, baptizing them in the name of the Father and the Son and the Holy Spirit, teaching them to observe all that I commanded you" (italics mine). The main imperative is to "make disciples"—literally, to create learners/students. This main command is a command to teach others to obey the Lord Jesus. If this is Jesus' final charge to the church—to create obedient students—then the foundation of our ministry must be that of preaching and teaching. Further, this foundation must consist of systematic, expository teaching, as we are instructed to "[teach others] to observe *all* that I commanded you" (italics mine). There is a stewardship entrusted to the church, not to pick and choose texts and topics, but to instruct believers in the totality of Jesus' teaching.

Expositional/Expository preaching and teaching is the discipline of delivering to the saints what was passed down from the Lord Jesus, and subsequently, from His apostles. We see that even the first church was "continually devoting themselves to the apostles' teaching" (Acts 2:42). If the command is to make disciples who are obedient to Christ's commands, then the only natural way to do it is to continuously expose them to the unadulterated biblical text. Upon leaving the church in Ephesus, the apostle Paul was confident that he had faithfully discharged his stewardship, stating, "Therefore I testify to you this, that I am innocent of the blood of all men. For I did not shrink from declaring to you the whole counsel of God" (Acts 20:26-27). It is the job of every preacher to stand before the people of God and faithfully discharge his ministry of reading, teaching, and exhorting with the Scriptures. As New England pastor Jonathan Edwards has declared, "The primary importance of the pastor is to be an expository preacher."[19]

Preach Passionately

Like many kids who grew up going to church, I have vivid memories of sitting in a hard-back wooden pew, listening to the pastor drone on for what seemed like hours. I would attribute this painful experience to young age and spiritual immaturity, but judging from the sagging faces and drooping eyes of my congregant neighbors, it's safe to say that I wasn't alone in my misery. But, according to D. Martyn Lloyd-Jones, "The preacher must never be dull, he must never be boring… a 'dull preacher' is a contradiction in terms; if he is dull he is not a preacher."[20] In fact, if a sermon is flat or boring, it's not the Bible's fault! Rather, it is the fault of the preacher. Further, Lloyd-Jones declared that true biblical preaching is "theology on fire!" However, so few preachers preach as though their hearts are burning within them. Why?

Passion is borne out of the soul, not out of the lungs. Louder preaching doesn't equal better preaching. At best, a loud yet dispassionate preacher comes across as insincere, if not angry. The listeners of this kind of preaching will only feel yelled-at, and likely shut down. From where, then, does the passion to preach originate? It radiates from the burning heart of God's servant.

The passion to preach faithfully comes from the conviction of the preacher. A passionate preacher is a man who is fully con-

---

[19] Lawson, *Famine in the Land*, 34.
[20] Lloyd-Jones, *Preaching & Preachers*, 87.

vinced and convicted by the Word of God. The preacher must first be transformed at the heart level before he can preach God's Word with passion. John Stott wrote, "The essential secret [of preaching] is not mastering certain techniques but being mastered by certain convictions. In other words, theology is more important than methodology."[21]

A preacher who is himself engaged only in the ritualistic exercise of instructing others has bypassed the essential step of being himself first transformed by the Word of God. Martyn Lloyd-Jones has said, "[The] preacher's first, and the most important task is to prepare himself, not his sermon."[22] The apostle Paul warns of this when he writes, "Therefore I run in such a way, as not without aim; I box in such a way, as not beating the air; but I buffet my body and make it my slave, lest possibly, after I have preached to others, I myself should be disqualified" (1 Cor. 9:26-27). The danger is that he will himself fail to be transformed by the very Scripture he is preaching. Addressing this danger, Richard Baxter laments, "many a preacher is now in hell, who hath a hundred times called upon his hearers to use the utmost care and diligence to escape it."[23]

Not only will an unconvinced, unconvicted, passionless preacher condemn himself, but he will also stunt the spiritual growth of the church. Mark Dever writes,

> To charge someone with the spiritual oversight of a church who doesn't in practice show a commitment to hear and to teach God's Word is to hamper the growth of the church, in essence allowing it to grow only to the level of the pastor. The church will slowly be conformed to the pastor's mind rather than to God's mind.[24]

A preacher who is himself committed to the Word of God in his own life will easily gush forth passion for it, because it holds a central place in his soul. Self-centered pastors think the church revolves around them, but Bible-centered pastors believe that all of

---

[21] Stott, *Between Two Worlds*, 92.

[22] Lloyd-Jones, *Preaching & Preachers*, 166.

[23] Richard Baxter, *The Reformed Pastor*. (1656, reprinted; Edinburgh: Banner of Truth, 1974), 53.

[24] Mark Dever, *Nine Marks of a Healthy Church*. (Wheaton, IL: Crossway, 2004), 42.

life revolves around God and His revealed Word! When this is their focus, they cannot help but set off the sprinklers with their white-hot passion!

The Charge and the Blessing

Perhaps the most direct command to preach in all of Scripture comes in Second Timothy 4:2—"Preach the word; be ready in season and out of season; reprove, rebuke, exhort, with great patience and instruction." This verse encapsulates the spirit of faithful expository preaching. It is important to remember that Jesus said that *He* would build His church (Matt. 16:18), not us. And if He is the One responsible for church growth, then we would do well to default to His message and His means. Sermons that prop up the authority of the pastor are not ultimately God-honoring; rather, we are to build our ministry on the One who will build the church, for Paul said, "we do not preach ourselves but Christ Jesus as Lord" (2 Cor. 4:5). And so, returning to 2 Timothy 4:2, I want to draw attention to three aspects of the verse.

First, Paul tells his disciple to "preach the word." This command dictates the method of delivery (preaching) and the subject matter (the Scriptures). Even if we had no other verses in the Bible charging us to preach, this verse could stand alone authoritatively. The Greek verb *kérusso* means to herald, to proclaim, or to preach. The content that is to be preached is "the word," namely the Scriptures. We are not called to have "conversations" or enter into religious "dialogue"—we are called to *preach*. What is to be our material? It is the living and active (Heb. 4:12), implanted Word of God "which is able to save your souls" (Jas. 1:21).

Second, once the command has come to preach the Scriptures, Paul intensifies the charge to preach it "in season and out of season," meaning—all the time! The preacher must be tireless in his effort to expound the Scriptures constantly, at every chance he gets. We must never grow bored, tired, or weary of the task of preaching the Word. Even on days when we just don't feel like it, we are encouraged: even when you're "in season" and things are going well, or "out of season" and things are challenging, even horrendous; we must be committed to preaching the Word of God.

Lastly, the final part of the verse contains a series of modifying commands which give greater detail to the task of preaching. This is more pragmatic, as Timothy is told to "reprove, rebuke, exhort, with great patience and instruction." While this is certainly not an exhaustive list, the idea is that no problem is too great that cannot be addressed with God's Word. Whether we are correcting error, calling out sin, or encouraging unto godliness, the Bible is a sharp sword that is expedient to accomplish all it sets out to do (Isa. 55:11), and is "able to judge the thoughts and intentions of the heart" (Heb. 4:12).

If you are impacted by nothing else in this chapter, then please consider 2 Timothy 4:2. This one verse is clear and direct enough for every pastor to begin heralding the word of truth, the gospel of salvation (Eph. 1:13), from their pulpits again. I encourage you; I implore you—preach the Word! There is nothing that will originate from within our brains or from TV or from the radio that will accomplish what needs to be accomplished in Christ's church.

Surely, the temptation will come to shirk this responsibility, and default to a more pragmatic approach to preaching—or worse—an attempt to water down your teaching to make it more palatable for people. The argument follows that the primary job of the pastor is to discern the spiritual needs of the congregation and provide them with practical solutions. However, issues like addiction, marriage problems, sexual sin, family turmoil, bad financial management, etc., stem from underdeveloped or faulty theology that simply cannot be fixed by a quick answer. It's like trying to mend a branch when the tree has root rot! Our complex problems go much deeper than we know and cannot be solved by our half-hearted self-help efforts. They must be addressed by the One who designed and built the human heart.

A Christian must be engaged in a prolonged immersion in biblical doctrine by which the Lord transforms the person at the heart level. Is it merely the exposure to verses and Bible terms? No, rather, it is the apprehension and implementation of God's very truth that changes people. Jesus Himself implored the Father to "sanctify them by the truth; Your Word is truth" (John 17:17).

We must never underestimate the dynamic power of the Word of God when it is rightly divided through faithful study and set on fire through passionate preaching. Mark Dever exhorts,

> Let a good expositional ministry be established and watch what happens. Forget what the experts say. Watch hungry people have their lives transformed as the living God speaks to them through the power of His Word.[25]

All the church growth strategies and clever communication techniques will never manufacture what God produces organically. The only way lost people are saved, weak believers are made strong, and mature saints are exhorted, is through biblical, expositional, and passionate preaching.

---

[25] Dever, *Nine Marks of a Healthy Church*, 54.

3

TILLING UP HARDENED SOIL

"Sow for yourselves righteousness; reap steadfast love;
break up your fallow ground, for it is the time to seek the Lord,
that He may come and rain righteousness upon you."
(Hosea 10:12, ESV)

My hometown is famous for two things: murder and scandal.

H.H. Holmes became known as America's first serial killer. Born Herman Webster Mudgett in 1861 in Gilmanton, New Hampshire, he moved to Chicago in 1893, where he would design and build a hotel specifically for the purpose of murdering people. When he was finally caught, he confessed to 27 murders, but some estimate he killed as many as 200 people. He was executed for his crimes in 1896. However, his infamy put his hometown on the map, and to this day, there is a sprawling exhibit in the Gilmanton historical society, showcasing his wicked escapades.

Less than five miles away from Holmes' birthplace lived the world-renowned writer, Grace Metalious. In 1956, she published *Peyton Place*, a fictitious novel chronicling the corrupt and immoral happenings of a small town in New Hampshire. The book became a runaway best seller. Full of incest, adultery, lust, and murder, much of the story bore an uncanny resemblance to real life events, and Metalious would bear public scorn from locals in her home town. After years of heavy drinking, she suffered from cirrhosis of the liver, and died in 1964 at the age of thirty-nine. In a sad twist or irony, her former residence is now the town winery.

The purpose of telling these two stories is to illustrate that, because of our lostness and depravity, we are not only drawn to sin, but we even showcase it. Left to our own devices, we will inevitably fall into sinful patterns that will destroy us. Furthermore, in a region once known for godliness, we have recently become infamous for our wickedness. And while the stories of H.H. Holmes and Grace Metalious are unique and fantastical, they serve to warn us of the presence of grotesque sin lurking even in our backyard.

But perhaps we're getting ahead of ourselves—we would do well to answer the question: what is *sin* and why does it matter?

The Problem of Sin

Generally speaking, the word *sin* is an archery term meaning "a failure to hit the mark"—to "sin" the target is to miss the bullseye. However, we understand it to be a religious word, reflecting moral or ethical failing. These days, however, we often treat sin as if it were some innocuous scuff in the cosmic continuum. We tend not to regard sin as a very serious thing. We misunderstand its significance and underestimate its power. Jerry Bridges astutely notes, "The entire concept of sin has virtually disappeared from our American culture at large and has been softened even within many of our churches, to accommodate modern sensibilities."[1] In doing so, however, not only have we missed the target, but we fail to realize *Whose* bullseye we have missed.

The Bible tells us that "In the beginning, God created the heavens and the earth" (Gen. 1:1) and "God saw everything that He had made, and behold, it was very good" (v. 31). The creation was perfect; built to His own standard. Then God created man and woman—Adam and Eve—and placed them into the utopia Garden of Eden, giving them freedom and dominion over all things (v. 26). Now, humankind was made in God's image and likeness (vv. 26-27), meaning that we were designed and built to be like Him and act as His representatives on earth. In doing so, we were to maintain God's perfect standard.

What is God's standard?

In short, God's standard is perfection. When giving the people of Israel His commands, God told them, "I am the Lord your God.

---

[1] Jerry Bridges, *Respectable Sins: Confronting the Sins We Tolerate.* (Colorado Springs, CO: NavPress, 2007), 18-19.

You must consecrate yourselves and be holy, because I am holy" (Lev. 11:44; 20:26; cf. 1 Pet. 1:16). When the Lord Jesus gave His Sermon on the Mount, He exhorted His followers once more, "You therefore must be perfect, as Your heavenly Father is perfect" (Matt. 5:48). God demands perfection.

Why does God demand perfection? Because He Himself is perfect.

The Bible teaches us much about the character and attributes of God. He is all-powerful (Gen. 18:14; Matt. 19:26), ever-present (Ps. 139:7-10; Jer. 23:23-24), all-knowing (Ps. 139:3-4; Job 37:16), unchanging (Ps. 102:25-27; Mal. 3:6), transcendent (Eph. 4:6), sovereign (Rev. 1:8), truthful (Titus 1:2; Heb. 6:18), etc. But the one attribute that seems elevated above all the others is God's holiness (Ps. 99:9; Isa. 1:4, 6:3). R.C. Sproul has wisely noted,

> The Bible never says that God is love, love, love; or mercy, mercy, mercy; or wrath, wrath, wrath; or justice, justice, justice. It does say that He is holy, holy, holy, that the whole earth is full of His glory.[2]

In Scripture, the threefold repetition "holy, holy, holy" establishes the gravity and prominence of the statement. In fact, the holiness of God is the prime feature of His perfect character, which encompasses all else that we know about Him. The word *holy* means "to set apart" but with regards to God, describes the height and depth of His perfection. In all ways, He is pure, righteous, and good. By comparison, in our attempt to be righteous, we jump like grasshoppers merely inches off the ground; God's holiness reaches the sun—93 million miles away.

In the Garden of Eden, God gave Adam a command not to eat from the tree of the knowledge of good and evil, and if he disobeyed, the punishment would be death (Gen. 2:17). But by chapter 3, Eve is deceived into believing the lie that eating from the forbidden tree would make them like God Himself (v. 5). They failed to trust God, disobeying Him.

Surely God cannot tolerate spiritual insurrection, can He? Can He simply look the other way, pretending that this "little gaffe" didn't happen? Of course not! His perfect character will not allow it. His

---

[2] R.C. Sproul, *The Holiness of God.* (Carol Stream, IL: Tyndale, 1985), 25.

righteousness will not permit it. His sense of justice cannot comprehend it. Why? Because if God were to fail to oppose and punish sin, He would be guilty of aiding and abetting sin, which would impugn His righteous character. May it never be!

Moreover, what we perceive to be a minor sin is actually a savage attack on the righteous character of God. And so, God punishes even the smallest infraction with severe and righteous judgment—an eternity in hell. James 2:10 says, "For whoever keeps the whole law and yet stumbles at one point, has become guilty of all of it." The Bible teaches that "the wages of sin is death" (Rom. 6:23), and further, that "all have sinned" (Rom. 3:23); none are truly righteous.

Once again, if the center bullseye is God's perfect holiness, then to *sin* the target is to fail to achieve His righteous standard. It is, in essence, to "fall short of the glory of God" (Rom. 3:23). But more than simply failing to hit a mark, the apostle John tells us that "sin is lawlessness" (1 John 3:4). Further, "[a sin] consists in doing, saying, thinking, or imagining, anything that is not in perfect conformity with the mind and law of God."[3] It is spiritual anarchy and rebellion. R.C. Sproul calls sin "cosmic treason."[4] More than being simply a series of flaws, missteps, peccadillos, or blunders, sin is a serious affront to the goodness and holiness of God. It is an attack on the throne of the King.

Sin is terminal, spiritual cancer—it hardens us, defiles us, degrades us, poisons us, enslaves us, kills us. But the greater impact falls not to us, but to God. Sin enrages Him, insults Him, assaults Him, undermines Him, attacks Him. And He responds with fierce wrath, burning anger, severe judgment, and eternal condemnation. To God, sin is not a light thing; it is an immense evil that is destined to be judged and eradicated.

But, if all are guilty of sinning against God, and His only course of action is divine condemnation, how is there any hope?

Enter Jesus Christ.

---

[3] J.C. Ryle, *Holiness: Its Nature, Hindrances, Difficulties, and Roots.* (1879, reprinted; Darlington: Evangelical Press, 1979), 2.
[4] Sproul, *The Holiness of God*, 115-116.

The Forgiveness of Sin through Christ

The Lord Jesus Christ, who is Himself God in human flesh (John 1:1-3, 14), came to earth and lived in perfect obedience to every law of God, thus perfectly fulfilling the divine standard. Jesus lived sinlessly (2 Cor. 5:21; Heb. 4:15; 1 Pet. 2:22), and thereby gave Himself up to be killed as an atoning sacrifice—a *propitiation*—for sin (1 John 2:2). Being the only acceptable sacrifice for sin, Jesus Christ died in the place of sinners as a *substitute* (1 Pet. 2:24), paying a ransom to the Father; *redeeming* us from the curse of the law (Gal. 3:13). Through the sacrificial death of Jesus, we can have our sins *forgiven* by God (Col. 2:13), and we are *justified*—declared pardoned and righteous by God, even though we're guilty and unrighteous (Rom. 3:28; Gal. 2:16).

It is the work of Jesus Christ on the cross that makes the forgiveness of sin possible for us. And not only forgiveness, but *reconciliation* to God—the restoration of relationship. Paul writes, "But God demonstrates His own love toward us, in that while we were yet sinners, Christ died for us. Much more then, having been justified by His blood, we shall be saved from the wrath of God through Him. For if while we were enemies, we were reconciled to God through the death of His Son, much more, having been reconciled, we shall be saved by His life" (Rom. 5:8-10).

This is why understanding and believing the gospel is so important. It is only by the death of Christ that we will find any hope of forgiveness for sin. All other attempts to "get right with God" are doomed to fail. Why? Because, by nature, we are sinful creatures, and when we try to accomplish anything of redeeming value, God turns up His nose and is repulsed by the gesture (Isa. 64:6). Any attempt we make to justify ourselves before Him is insulting and futile. Only the perfect work of Jesus Christ on our behalf is pleasing to the Father.

Sin in the Camp

So many Christian leaders and churchgoers are laboring hard to bring about God's blessing in hopes of revival, but all their efforts are completely useless if there is "sin in the camp." In the book of Joshua, we read about the great conquests of Israel to capture the Promised Land. Their spirits were soaring and religious zeal was at an all-time high. Joshua, the commander of the Israelite army, was promised by God that he would have sustained victory over their enemies as long as Israel remained in obedience to God's commands. All was going well until one man sinned.

In Joshua chapter 7, we read about a soldier named Achan, who, while collecting the spoils of war, stole some of the devoted items and hid them in his tent. Because of this greedy action, "the anger of the Lord burned against the people of Israel" (v. 1). Suddenly, Israel was losing, and the enemy managed to drive the army back, killing thirty-six Israelite soldiers. This was a disheartening blow. Joshua tore his clothes in mourning and cried out to God for an answer. Why was God angry with them and withholding victory?

The answer comes in verses 10-11, "The Lord said to Joshua, 'Get up! Why have you fallen on your face? Israel has sinned; they transgressed my covenant that I commanded them; they have taken some of the devoted things; they have stolen and lied and put them among their own belongings." One seemingly tiny sin, committed by one soldier out of hundreds of thousands, brought about the wrath of God on all the people. Joshua investigates and finds Achan guilty, and after confessing to his transgression, Achan and his whole family are put to death and burned (vv. 22-26). The punishment is severe, but the message couldn't be clearer: God has absolutely no tolerance for sin.

How many of our churches are filled with believers who are wracked with unconfessed sin? How many unbelievers are masquerading as Christians, lying to themselves as well as the congregation? How much of God's burning anger is resting on our heads, yet we have the audacity to ask God to bless our endeavors?

But if this is true, and our camp is filled with Achans who have sinned against God, how can we proceed and pray for true revival? We've already seen that we cannot simply "make things right" through our own efforts. No amount of charity work will do. No number of Saturday nights at soup kitchens will do the trick. No number of hours raking the lawns of the elderly will accomplish the atonement needed for the forgiveness of our sins. What we need is to access the atoning work of Jesus Christ. We need *His* righteousness. We need *His* sinlessness. We need the ransom that only *He* can pay.

And therefore, we need genuine repentance.

The Need for Repentance

During the midst of Israel's apostasy, the Lord used the prophets to command the people to return to Him. In Hosea's prophecy, the hardness of the people's hearts is compared to that of hardened soil, whereby the Lord commands them: "break up your fallow ground, for it is the time to seek the Lord, that He may come and rain righteousness upon you" (Hos. 10:12; cf. Jer. 4:3). They were to put their hand to the plow and dig up their own hearts, sowing righteousness in its place. How was this to be done? What was this image to conjure up for them? It was to be the work of repentance.

In the Old Testament, a word commonly used for repentance is *shub*, meaning "to change a course of action, to turn away, or to turn back."[5] The word was often used to refer to a geographical return, as in the return of God's people from exile. However, it was also used to articulate a spiritual return to God.

But the New Testament is dominated by the Greek word *metanoia*, which literally means "afterthought" and has to do with a change of mind. Sinclair Ferguson defines repentance as "a change of mind that leads to a change of lifestyle."[6] Puritan Thomas Watson notes that "Repentance is a grace of God's Spirit whereby a sinner is inwardly humbled and visibly reformed."[7] John MacArthur offers an even more nuanced definition: "It is a redirection of the human will, a purposeful decision to forsake all unrighteousness and pursue righteousness instead."[8]

In Luke 15, Jesus tells the story of the prodigal son; a beautiful picture of repentance and restoration. The son, who, after squandering his father's inheritance and living among pigs, has a change of mind; a change of heart. Jesus retells, "But when he came to

---

[5] Sinclair Ferguson, *The Grace of Repentance*. (Wheaton, IL: Crossway, 2010), 15-16.
[6] Ibid., 18.
[7] Thomas Watson, *The Doctrine of Repentance*. (1668, reprinted; Edinburgh: Banner of Truth Trust, 1987), 18.
[8] John MacArthur, *The Gospel According to Jesus*. (Grand Rapids, MI: Zondervan, 1988), 178.

himself" (v. 17) the son decided to return to the father and ask forgiveness.

The Elements of Repentance

While defining repentance is helpful and necessary, it will be of even more value to us if we understand the various elements of repentance. It's important to note that simply feeling sorry for sin is not by itself repentance. Often times, the kneejerk reaction of sorrow is tied more to the fact that a person has been caught and has to suffer penalty; not that one is sorry over the sin itself. And so, in order to shepherd us into a right understanding of repentance, we must see that there are three main elements.

The first is *intellectual.* At a certain point, one needs to recognize that they've sinned. God's command has been transgressed and rebellion is taking place. It's a mental acknowledgment; a realization. This is what it means to "come to your senses" (cf. Luke 15:17). After all, the New Testament Greek word *metanoia* pertains mostly to the mind, as it comes to the awareness of sin and experiences a change in thinking. King David, after sinning with Bathsheba, wrote "I acknowledged my sin to you, and did not cover my iniquity" (Ps. 32:5). John MacArthur writes, "repentance begins with a recognition of sin—the understanding that we are sinners, that our sin is an affront to a holy God, and more precisely, that we are personally responsible for our own guilt."[9] One of the biggest problems we face is an inability, even an unwillingness, to recognize and admit our own guilt over sin. However, we must call it what it is and be prepared to follow through with what we have purposed in our mind.

The second is *emotional.* This is where the feelings enter into the equation. It's important to note that remorse over our current situation isn't necessarily a sign of true repentance, but there needs to be genuine sorrow over our sin (2 Cor. 7:9-11) and over transgressing God's law. As a Christian believer, we should be deeply troubled that we have offended God with our transgression. Further, we have broken communion with Him. Again, David declares to the Lord, "For you will not delight in sacrifice, or I would give it… The sacrifices of God are a broken spirit; a broken and contrite heart, O God, you

---

[9] Ibid., 179.

will not despise" (Ps. 51:16a-17). God wants us broken and mourning over our sin. That is the mark of true repentance. But there is still more.

The third is *volitional*. This is an act of the will. Surely the first step is the confession of sin; working in league with the first part—the intellect—to realize and own up to the sin. Louis Berkhof notes that there is "a volitional element, consisting in a change of purpose, an inward turning away from sin, and a disposition to seek pardon and cleansing."[10]

When King Solomon set out to dedicate the new temple, the Lord came to him and affirmed the promise of the covenant, that if the people obeyed, they would receive divine blessing. The Lord told him, "If My people who are called by my name humble themselves, and pray and seek my face and *turn from their wicked ways*, then I will hear from heaven and will forgive their sin and heal their land" (2 Chron. 7:14, emphasis mine). A definite turning must occur, otherwise there is no visible evidence of repentance (see Matt. 3:8)!

But before we proceed too far, we must remember that it is not by repentance that we are saved—it is by faith alone in Jesus Christ (Rom. 3:28; Gal. 2:16; Eph. 2:8-9). In fact, Richard Owen Roberts writes, "Repentance is not the entry ticket into the kingdom of God, but it is a condition of citizenship."[11] However, the link between the two is unbreakable, as "repentance and faith are wed together, never to be divorced. True repentance does not stand alone but is always linked with true faith. True faith does not stand alone but is always linked with true repentance."[12] By faith, a step away from the rebellion of sin is also a step toward obedience to God. Louis Berkhof writes,

> [T]rue repentance never exists except in conjunction with faith, while, on the other hand, wherever there is true faith, there is also real repentance. The two are but different aspects of the same turning,—a turning away from sin in the

---

[10] Louis Berkhof, *Systematic Theology*. (Grand Rapids, MI: Eerdmans, 1939), 486.
[11] Richard Owen Roberts, *Repentance: The First Word of the Gospel*. (Wheaton, IL: Crossway, 2002), 28.
[12] Ibid., 68.

direction of God… the two cannot be separated; they are simply complementary parts of the same process.[13]

By faith, we recognize and trust that God is who He says He is and what He has revealed is good, right, and true. By faith, we repent of transgressing His perfect law. By faith, we trust that what He has promised to those who obey is greater than the short-sighted kick we get from sin, as a lifetime of unrepentant sin condemns us to hell. By faith, we repent; our repentance is a fruit of our faith. So there can be no confusion, Roberts asserts, "Both repentance and faith are mandatory to salvation. You must turn from your sin in order to turn to Jesus Christ. You cannot turn to Christ unless you have turned from your sin. Repentance and faith belong together. Any attempt to separate them is a grievous mistake."[14]

What is God's promise to us with regards to repentance? "If we confess our sins, he is faithful and just to forgive us our sins and to cleanse us from all unrighteousness" (1 John 1:9). The promise is two-fold; He will forgive our sins, removing our transgressions from us (cf. Ps. 103:12; Col. 2:14) and will cleanse us, washing us from the inside out, restoring our souls (Ps. 51:7; Eph. 5:26-27; Titus 3:5). While sin must be confessed because of its sheer offense to God, He is also gracious in desiring to forgive and restore us.

But the cleansing process can be difficult.

Killing Your Sin

Not many people are drawn to the idea of "killing" when it comes to their spirituality. But the Bible uses very graphic language to describe the process by which we are to fight against our own sin. In Romans 8:13, the apostle Paul writes, "For if you live according to the flesh you will die, but if by the Spirit you put to death the deeds of the body, you will live." His instruction to believers who are struggling against sin is to "put to death" their sinful deeds. Older English translations referred to this act as "mortification." Puritan

---

[13] Berkhof, *Systematic Theology*, 487.
[14] Roberts, *Repentance*, 70.

John Owen writes, "Mortification is the soul's vigorous opposition to self, wherein sincerity is most evident."[15] It is the killing of that which eats away at your soul, desiring to kill you. And the mortification of your own sin begins with repentance, but continues with an all-out spiritual warfare of the soul.

How do we fight this life-long battle against our own sinful natures? What does this warfare look like? Space does not permit me to exhaust this topic. But let me suggest a few exhortations:

First, your warfare must be *deliberate.* No one drifts toward godliness. The fight for godliness is done purposefully, as we're fighting against our own nature. As you become more self-aware regarding God's righteousness and your own sinfulness, there must be a conscious willingness to oppose sinful desires and submit to the will of God. Jesus described this kind of commitment when He said, "If anyone would come after me, let him deny himself and take up his cross daily and follow me" (Luke 9:23). The Christian life is a deliberate, daily exercise in self-denial for the purpose of chasing Christlikeness.

Second, your warfare must be *radical.* Godliness is not accomplished through passivity. Anything short of complete obedience is an exercise in disobedience. Nowhere in the Gospels does Jesus grant eternal life to anyone who was willing only to commit a portion of their life to Him (Matt. 19:16-22; Luke 9:57-62). With Jesus, it's all or nothing. When God commanded King Saul to wipe out the Amalekites in 1 Samuel 15, He was not at all vague. Saul was to kill every "man and woman, child and infant, ox and sheep, camel and donkey" (v. 3). But after defeating their army, Saul spared the Amalekite king Agag, as well as some of the best livestock. When the prophet Samuel heard that Saul had taken Agag alive and showcased him as a trophy, Samuel was furious! After confronting Saul on his sin of disobedience, the Bible says that "Samuel hacked Agag to pieces before the Lord in Gilgal" (v. 33). God demands nothing short of complete and radical obedience.

Third, your warfare must be *spiritual.* With all this talking of "killing" and "hacking," we must be reminded that "the weapons of

---

[15] John Owen, *On the Mortification of Sin in Believers* in Kelly M. Kapic and Justin Taylor, eds., *Overcoming Sin and Temptation.* (Wheaton, IL: Crossway, 2006), 66.

our warfare are not of the flesh" (2 Cor. 10:4), but rather, are spiritual in nature (cf. Eph. 6:12). We don't physically attack others, nor do we harm ourselves. Our warfare is that of aggression against the impulses of our hearts that rebel against God and hijack our efforts to live for Him. We fight thoughts. We fight unbelief. We fight evil desires. We fight ideologies that stand in opposition to God. Our enemies are spiritual—the world, the flesh, and the devil (Eph. 2:2-3)—and we must fight with spiritual weapons.

Lastly, your warfare must be *tireless*. The Christian life should not be lived in short bursts. Jerry Bridges once said, "The Christian life… [is] an obstacle course of marathon length."[16] We are called to persevere, overcoming obstacles, and pressing on to the end. Jesus said, "The one who endures to the end will be saved" (Matt. 24:13; cf. 1 Cor. 9:24-27). What good would it be to fight sin for a few years, only to slide back into your former condition at the end of your life? Is God glorified by such a failing? Absolutely not. This life as a Christian consists of nothing less than "an ongoing, dogged, persistent refusal to compromise with sin."[17]

Calling Out Sins by Name

Most people, if they're honest with themselves, will admit that they are a sinner. But it seems a much more penetrating thing to examine oneself and get specific. In his timeless work, *The Doctrine of Repentance*, Puritan pastor Thomas Watson wrote, "A wicked man acknowledges he is a sinner in general. He confesses sin by wholesale… whereas a true convert acknowledges his particular sins."[18] It is not enough to admit that we are sinners; we must get down and dirty and confess them to God by name.

First, we must deal with our *individual* sins. These are specific sins like lying, stealing, gossip, slander, adultery, sexual immorality, blasphemy, etc. (see Mark 7:21-22; 1 Cor. 6:9-10; Gal. 5:19-21; Rev. 21:8; etc.). Since God desires us to be holy, there must not even be a hint of sin unconfessed (see Eph. 5:3). Whenever you transgress

---

[16] Jerry Bridges, *Trusting God Even When Life Hurts*. (Colorado Springs, CO: NavPress, 1998), 198.

[17] Ferguson, *The Grace of Repentance*, 25.

[18] Watson, *The Doctrine of Repentance*, 30.

God's law, the sin must be confessed—quickly, completely, humbly, and earnestly. Don't wait around and let the sin fester within you. Further, there are many sins that are indwelling; they are long-standing habitual sins that must not only be confessed, but uprooted. A.W. Tozer illustrates this struggle perfectly:

> The ancient curse will not go out painlessly; the tough old miser within us will not lie down and die in obedience to our command. He must be torn out of our heart like a plant from the soil; he must be extracted in agony and blood like a tooth from the jaw. He must be expelled from our soul by violence, as Christ expelled the money changers from the temple.[19]

Dear Christian, we simply cannot afford to dabble with sin. It must be confronted head-on, confessed sincerely, and fought vigorously (1 Pet. 2:11).

Then, we must acknowledge our *corporate* sins. Now, this may seem a bit odd at first, but we must remember that sin does not just affect individuals only; it affects whole churches, as well as whole communities, regions, and nations. Just like with Achan, sin within a body of believers can have toxic effects. It destroys unity, corrupts consciences, causes members to stumble, and undermines the unity of the Spirit (Eph. 4:3). Hence, the need for church purity (cf. Matt. 18:15-17; 1 Cor. 5:1-13). And so, "repentance [must be] worked out both inwardly and outwardly in entire communities of believers."[20]

Often times, certain sins can become so entrenched in a community, it may take years or decades to unseat. When the culture of a town or a region becomes so corrupt, the collective conscience is dulled. Invariably, gossip and slander will find its way into the church. Town politics will find its way into the church. Sexual immorality, or the tolerance of immorality, will find its way into the church. Bigotry and hatred will find its way into the church. These are cultural sins that bang down church doors in every New England community. Thankfully, we know that "the gates of hell cannot pre-

---

[19] A.W. Tozer, *The Pursuit of God*. (1948, republished; Camp Hill, PA: Wing Spread, 2006), 29.

[20] Ferguson, *The Grace of Repentance*, 39.

vail" against the church (Matt. 16:18)! However, as David L. Smith notes regarding the nature of sin,

> [O]ne must not confine oneself to individuals. An indictment must be returned against corporate sin… all human entities have been touched by evil, institutions and societies included. Because they are constituted by sinful people, they too are sinful. When institutions—whether political, economic, religious, or educational—oppress, exploit, or manipulate people, Christians must speak out against them. We should remember God's punishment of the Hebrew people in Old Testament times because they allowed social injustice and failed to take any steps against the situation… God has not been lenient in regard to corporate sin, and we need to follow the prophets of the eighth and seventh century (B.C.) period in condemning such transgression.[21]

When a Christian community is vigilant and quick to oppose and repent of any and all sin, they may be enabled to walk in righteousness, honor God, and thereby fulfill their mission.

Sanctification and Christian Living

In his first letter to the Thessalonians, Paul declared in no uncertain terms: "For this is the will of God, your sanctification" (4:3). We can busy ourselves with all kinds of ministry, set lofty goals, or devote ourselves to a lifetime of prayer, but if we are not being sanctified, we are operating outside the will of God.

So, what is *sanctification*? It is the process of becoming holy, set apart or separated, consecrated to God. And in the context of the Bible, it is the separation away from sin and worldliness, and unto holiness and godliness. In fact, we are called to "be imitators of God, as beloved children" (Eph. 5:1). Contrary to the common misconception regarding holiness, it must be said that "Holiness is not a series of do's and don'ts, but conformity to the character of God and obedience to the will of God."[22] In essence, we are trying to be like

---

[21] David L. Smith, *With Willful Intent: A Theology of Sin.* (Wheaton, IL: Bridgepoint, 1994), 412.

[22] Jerry Bridges, *The Pursuit of Holiness.* (Colorado Springs, CO: NavPress, 1978), 68.

the Lord, who is Himself represented to us perfectly in Jesus Christ (Col. 1:15; Heb. 1:3). So, sanctification is the process by which we grow to be more like Christ. Once again, we are told, "But put on the Lord Jesus Christ, and make no provision for the flesh, to gratify its desires" (Rom. 13:14).

As stated previously, not all of Christianity is repentance and the killing of sin. In fact, Jesus warns of the danger of allowing evil back into your heart once it has been expelled (Matt. 12:43-45; Luke 11:24-26). It is not enough to confess sin and strive against it, simply holding the line. You must reinforce your life with godliness.

In Ephesians 4, the apostle Paul introduces the church to a principle of sanctification whereby the believer is to "put off your old self, which belongs to your former manner of life and is corrupt through deceitful desires" (v. 22); and, in its place, "put on the new self, created after the likeness of God in true righteousness and holiness" (v. 24). This two-handed approach to sanctification—the "put off/put on" principle—is what is prescribed for growing in godliness.

In applying Paul's method, the believer is to identify and confess sin, while praying for God to help root out and replace it with the corresponding fruit of the Spirit (Eph. 5:22-23). For example, in the case of slandering another person, confess the sin and ask God to help find ways to build that person up and exhort them. In the case of pride and self-righteousness, confess the sin and enlist the help of the Lord to teach you the ways of humility.

Living a godly life is not optional. Growing in Christlikeness is not optional. In fact, Jesus Himself tells His disciples that if their lives are not bearing the fruit of righteousness, it is evidence that they do not belong to Him and will eventually be cut off and thrown into the fire (John 15:1-8)! The author of Hebrews tells us that we are to "strive for peace with everyone, and *for the holiness without which no one will see the Lord*" (Heb. 12:14, emphasis mine). Did you catch that? If you are not chasing after holiness in your Christian walk, you will have no chance of seeing the Lord in eternity. Why? Because you will prove that your faith is not genuine (Jas. 2:14-17).

There is no room for spiritual laziness. Paul describes the Christian life as a race and a boxing match (1 Cor. 9:24-27). It's a life that will be marked with trials and suffering. But we are encouraged: "Since therefore Christ suffered in the flesh, arm yourselves with the same way of thinking, for whoever has suffered in the flesh has ceased from sin, so as to live for the rest of the time in the flesh no longer for human passions but for the will of God" (1 Pet. 4:1-2, ESV). We must be contenders for the faith (Jude 3), those who labor tirelessly for goodness, righteousness, and holiness. Writing about the challenge of striving for holiness, J.C. Ryle notes,

> There are thousands of men and women who go to churches and chapels every Sunday, and call themselves Christians. Their names are in the baptismal register. They are reckoned Christians while they live. They are married with a Christian marriage service. They mean to be buried as Christians when they die. But you never see any 'fight' about their religion! Of spiritual strife and exertion and conflict and self-denial and watching and warring they know literally nothing at all.[23]

The Call to Laboring in Your Own Soul

We can pray for revival and hope for a resurgence of Christianity in New England, but if we do not "press on toward the goal for the prize of the upward call of God in Christ Jesus" (Phil. 3:14), then we will forfeit any potential blessing that God might have for us up here. And while it may seem presumptuous to say that He will not act in this way—as if we're dictating terms to God—the weight of Scripture reinforces this truth. God does not bless disobedience. He does not honor wickedness. Rather, "We need to have a revival of preaching against sin," writes David L. Smith. "The church seems to have lost its concern that those who persist in their sinful condition will go to hell and experience eternal loss... One reason for the decline of the church in our society is a lessening of evangelistic fervor. Unless and until we can restore a practical concern for the redemption of the lost, decline will continue and people will continue to flock into hell."[24]

---

[23] Ryle, *Holiness*, 51.
[24] Smith, *With Willful Intent*, 410.

We cannot be so arrogant to think that we can continue on, business-as-usual, if we are living in open rebellion to the Lord. Left unchecked and unrepented of, our sin will utterly destroy us and God will give us over to our own depraved condition (Rom. 1:18-32). Jesus said, "Whoever does not take his cross and follow me is not worthy of me" (Matt. 10:38), and whoever does not "come after me cannot be my disciple" (Luke 14:27). Jesus demands a life of devotion and self-denial for the purpose of godliness. He demands obedience (Matt. 28:20; John 14:15, 23). He calls us to "be holy, as your heavenly Father is holy" (Matt. 5:48; cf. Lev. 20:26; 1 Pet. 1:16). He honors faithfulness, humility, and holiness.

But isn't it all worth it? Would you not give anything to live like your Lord once you were saved? Are the promises of God not good, right, and true? God has loved us so much that He gave His only Son as a sacrifice for our sin. Is our love and obedience not a small token of thankfulness for so great a gift? Is even the possibility of God reviving New England worth consecrating ourselves to His service?

Will it be difficult? Yes. Will it take effort and self-examination? Yes. Will it take humility? Absolutely. But if we are to lead people to return to God, repentance and faith are absolutely essential, and they are costly. Let us make no mistake:

> Surely a Christian should be willing to give up anything which stands between him and heaven. A religion that costs nothing is worth nothing! A cheap Christianity, without a cross, will prove in the end a useless Christianity, without a crown.[25]

Till up the hardened soil of your own heart, and cultivate the fruitful crops of repentance and righteousness. If we do not deal with the problem of sin, there will surely be no spiritual revival in New England.

---

[25] Ryle, *Holiness*, 70.

4

TEARING DOWN THE FENCES

"If therefore there is any encouragement in Christ,
if there is any consolation of love, if there is any fellowship of the Spirit,
if any affection and compassion,
make my joy complete by being of the same mind,
maintaining the same love, united in spirit, intent on one purpose."
Philippians 2:1-2, NASB

Robert Frost, a native New Englander, published his poem, "Mending Wall" in 1914; a sort-of literary commentary on rural New England life from the perspective of a farmer. In the poem, two neighboring farmers meet in the Spring, walking along the stone wall which marks out their property line. The narrator questions the purpose of the wall, but his neighbor only responds with the proverbial maxim, "Good fences make good neighbors."

While Frost did not originate this line, he no doubt made it famous. The sentiment seems to undergird the New England temperament, as it explores the tension between all communal relationships in the Northeast. New Englanders are reserved and guarded, tentative and contemplative, self-reliant and proud, principled and often stubborn. While not necessarily cold, we are not known for our "Northern hospitality," rather, we keep to ourselves. Despite our desire for friends, we struggle to embrace communal living. But for those who desire more engagement, there are societies and clubs. And for those with a more "religious" bent, there are churches.

Lots of churches.

In fact, every town is peppered with old, white churches, many of them only a quarter filled with aged people desperate for community and purpose. But in many cases, the spiritual health of those churches is dire. Due to scarce regular attendance, new visitors are welcomed with awkward zeal, and quickly made "members" at the first sign of interest. However, when trouble arises, a churchgoer may use their tithe and attendance as a bargaining chip, extorting the church to cater to their small demands. And so, the local church becomes a social gathering, built on the wants and needs of the individual members.

The average New England church is not completely self-focused, however, there is a general sense of "doing good" for the local community. The church may engage in various philanthropic endeavors, serving general felt needs in the town. And while, on the surface, this seems altruistic and commendable, many of our churches are devoid of any real sense of Christian identity and true godliness. Any "evangelistic" efforts are more to win people to the church itself, not necessarily to Christ. As the saving gospel is lost in obscurity, their collective identity is built on the *notion* of "church," and members are merely cogs in the hand-cranked machine that keeps the decrepit institution propped upright. But, in truth, there is very little of Jesus Christ, and church membership has nearly become a meaningless thing.

So, what must be done?

In short, the *identity* of the church must be rediscovered in order that the *mission* of the church may be reignited. And so, we will explore the outworking of this in the next two chapters.

First, let's examine the *identity* of the church.

Jesus Christ and the Identity of the Church

The first place the concept of "church" is mentioned in the New Testament is by Jesus in Matthew 16. In the latter part of His three-year ministry, Jesus and His disciples gathered in the district of Caesarea Philippi, approximately 25 miles north of the Sea of Galilee. Once together, Jesus begins to ask questions of His disciples. Central to His inquiry is the question, "Who do people say that the Son of Man is" (v. 13)? In essence, He's asking them, "Who do people think I am?" They give a series of answers, as some thought He was John the Baptist, others thought He was Elijah or Jeremiah, or one of the other prophets reincarnated (v. 14). But then

Jesus poses the question to them: "Who do *you* say that I am?" (v. 15, emphasis added). I often imagine that there might have been a brief pause, the disciples looking at one another, nervous about giving a wrong answer. But then Peter pipes up and says, "You are the Christ, the Son of the living God" (v. 16). Immediately, Jesus responds positively, affirming Peter's profession, "Blessed are you, Simon Bar-Jonah! For flesh and blood has not revealed this to you, but my Father who is in heaven" (v. 17).

The nature of Jesus' question was to flesh out their understanding of who He is—His identity. Not only does Peter correctly identify Jesus as "the Christ"—the long-awaited Jewish Messiah, but he identifies Him as "the son of the living God"—a declaration of deity.[1] Based on his confession of faith in Jesus as Lord and Savior, He responds by praising the Father, as this information could not be fully discerned and confessed apart from a divine work of God. The confession is a sovereignly revealed confession.

Not only does Jesus joyfully bless Peter for his confession, He also announces the establishment of a new entity; a group of believers who will share Peter's same confession. In verse 18, Jesus declares, "And I tell you, you are Peter, and on this rock I will build my church, and the gates of hell shall not prevail against it." The Roman Catholic Church has wrongly interpreted this verse to mean that the church will be built on *Peter*, rather than on Peter's *confession of faith.* We know, in fact, that Jesus Himself is the cornerstone; the rock on which the entire church is built (see 1

---

[1] While some have questioned the extent to Peter's understanding, R.T. France asserts that "it is a powerful reminder that the God with whom Jesus is here being connected is not a philosophical abstraction but the dynamic God of Israel's faith and history." *The Gospel of Matthew.* NICNT. (Grand Rapids, MI: Eerdmans, 2007), 619. D.A. Carson concurs that "'Son of God' may well have had purely messianic significance in Peter's mind... even though it came to indicate divinity." "Matthew" in *The Expositor's Bible Commentary.* Volume 8 (Grand Rapids, MI: Zondervan, 1984), 365-366. However, John MacArthur writes, "Now, at last, the truth of Jesus' divinity and messiahship was established in their minds beyond question... God's own Spirit had now imbedded the truth indelibly in their hearts." Matthew 16-23. *The MacArthur New Testament Commentary.* (Chicago, IL: Moody, 1988), 21.

Pet. 2:6-8; cf. Isa. 28:16; Ps. 118:22).[2] While Jesus Christ is the cornerstone of the church, believers are added "as living stones" (1 Pet. 2:5).

And so, the formulation of this "church" (the Greek word *ekklésia* means "assembly") will be built squarely on the person of Jesus Christ, and entrance into this believing group will be based on the God-given faith of its members. Jesus Himself is the head (Eph. 5:23b; Col. 1:18, 2:19) and the believers form His body (1 Cor. 12:12-31). Therefore, the core identity of every believer is found in the Lord Jesus Christ. Speaking about the church, Mark Dever writes, "[it is] a regular assembly of people who profess and give evidence that they have been saved by God's grace alone through faith alone in Christ alone to the glory of God alone."[3] While Jesus announced the coming of the church in Matthew 16, we see its fulfilment in Acts 2.

The Birth of Christian Community

Six weeks after the resurrection of Jesus Christ, the Holy Spirit descended on the believers in Jerusalem who were praying and worshiping God during the Feast of Pentecost. This assembly of believers had gathered "all together in one place" (Acts 2:1). Suddenly, the Spirit burst into their gathering, and "tongues as of fire… rested on each one of them. And they were all filled with the Holy Spirit and began to speak with other tongues as the Spirit was giving them utterance" (vv. 3-4). We understand this to be the first occurrence of the indwelling of believers by the Holy Spirit. In this pivotal act, the believers were "sealed in Him with the Holy Spirit of promise, who is given as a pledge of our inheritance, with a view to the redemption of God's own possession, to the praise of His glory" (Eph. 1:13b-14). In other

---

[2] Contrary to the Roman Catholic doctrine, it has been noted that "When the image of a foundation stone is used in relation to the Christian church elsewhere in the NT, that stone is Jesus himself, not Peter." R.T. France, *The Gospel of Matthew*. NICNT. (Grand Rapids, MI: Eerdmans, 2007), 622. Further, "there is no mention of any successors of Peter; whatever position is assigned to him is personal and not transmissible to those who would succeed him." Leon Morris, *The Gospel According to Matthew*. Pillar New Testament Commentary (Grand Rapids, MI: Eerdmans, 1992), 424.

[3] Mark Dever, *A Display of God's Glory*. (Washington, DC: 9Marks, 2001), 50.

words, the saving work of Jesus Christ accomplished on the cross was permanently applied to their souls, as God had sealed them with His irrevocable mark of ownership and protection. In this one act, the first believers were "baptized into one body" (1 Cor. 12:13).

Very quickly, this final work of God in salvation spread to all believers "in Jerusalem, and in all Judea and Samaria, and even to the remotest part of the earth" (Acts 1:8). From that point on, and for today, regeneration, faith, and indwelling comes to every believer at conversion.[4] But we get a very unique view into a crucial and transitional period in history, as the grace of the New Covenant is poured out on the church, and the body of Christ is formed. In examining Acts 2, we are able to see the church in its infancy, and we notice key elements that were paramount in the beginning.

Fellowship: Sharing Life Together

While the first gathering at Pentecost may have been as few as 120 believers (Acts 1:15), the new Spirit-filled group quickly took to the streets, preaching the gospel (Acts 2:6-11). However, it was the event of Peter's sermon (2:14-36) that brought about the adding of three thousand new believers to the church (v. 41)—those who would repent of their sins (v. 38) and believe the gospel (v. 44). It was this first group of Christians that got to experience the blessing of true fellowship.

We read:

> They were continually devoting themselves to the apostles' teaching and to fellowship, to the breaking of bread and to prayer. Everyone kept feeling a sense of awe; and many

---

[4] While some charismatic believers maintain that Acts 2 proves the existence of a second blessing occurring later to secure salvation—the "baptism in the Holy Spirit"—it must be understood that this is not normative in the conversion experience. Even continuationist scholar Wayne Grudem notes, "as far as the apostle Paul was concerned, *baptism in the Holy Spirit occurred at conversion*... [and] therefore, must refer to the activity of the Holy Spirit at the beginning of the Christian life when he gives us a new spiritual life (in regeneration) and cleanses us and gives us a clear break with the power and love of sin (the initial state of sanctification)." *Systematic Theology: An Introduction to Christian Doctrine.* (Grand Rapids, MI: Zondervan, 1994), 768-769. Emphasis original.

wonders and signs were taking place through the apostles. And all those who had believed were together and had all things in common; and they began selling their property and possessions and were sharing them with all, as anyone might have need. Day by day continuing with one mind in the temple, and breaking bread from house to house, they were taking their meals together with gladness and sincerity of heart, praising God and having favor with all the people. And the Lord was adding to their number day by day those who were being saved. (Acts 2:42-47)

While this first account does not serve as a *formula* for church fellowship, it does showcase various *principles* that will certainly be present in every Christian gathering. Four main elements emerge from this passage: a devotion to biblical instruction, fellowship, the breaking of bread (some believe this refers to the Lord's Supper), and prayer. For our purposes here, and without diminishing the others, I want to focus on fellowship.

The Greek word *koinōnia* is a unique word. Generally, it can be thought of as "a common life together."[5] But, in truth, the word is more nuanced than that. Literally, the word means "what is held in common."[6] It "denotes 'participation,' 'fellowship,' [especially] with a close bond. It expresses a two-sided relation… [and] may be on either the giving or the receiving."[7]

In the context of Acts 2, David Peterson notes that *koinōnia* may be referring "to material blessings, as described in vv. 44-45, where we are told that the believers had everything in common (*koina*). Yet this sharing was clearly a practical expression of the new relationship experienced together through a common faith in Christ (cf. vv. 38-41)."[8] This is more than Sunday morning lobby-talk over

---

[5] John MacArthur, *The Master's Plan for the Church.* (Chicago, IL: Moody, 2008), 72.

[6] David L. Smith, *All God's People: A Theology of the Church.* (Wheaton, IL: Bridgepoint, 1996), 345.

[7] Gerhard Kittel, *Theological Dictionary of the New Testament. Volume III.* Translated by Geoffrey W. Bromiley. (Grand Rapids, MI: Eerdmans, 1965), 798.

[8] David G. Peterson, *The Acts of the Apostles. Pillar New Testament Commentary* (Grand Rapids, MI: Eerdmans, 2009), 160.

coffee; there is a spiritual bond which permeates every selfless action. With Acts 2 in mind, let's examine the biblical aspects of *koinōnia*.

Communion with God

In His high priestly prayer, Jesus prays to the Father that He might unify all believers in Him based on the unity that exists between the Father and the Son. He prays "that they may all be one; even as You, Father, are in Me, and I in You, that they also may be in Us… that they may be one, just as We are one" (John 17:21-22). True unity among all believers is grounded in the unity that exits within the Godhead—between the Father and the Son, but also with the Spirit.

Twice in the New Testament, we encounter the phrase "fellow-ship of the Spirit" (2 Cor. 13:14; Phil. 2:1). It implies that true fellowship is derived from and perpetuated by the person of the Holy Spirit. In fact, the church is charged with "being diligent to preserve the unity of the Spirit in the bond of peace" (Eph. 4:3). While our own fellowship with God through the Spirit is personal, it also binds us in a common experience, acting as our basis for Christian unity. Jerry Bridges notes, "Without this relationship with God, there can be no spiritual relationship with one another."[9] We can have true fellowship with one another because, as born again believers, we have true fellowship with God.

Unity with Other Believers

The unity that originates in the triune God extends to believers and expands throughout the whole church. The first church shared this unity, as "the congregation of those who believed were of one heart and soul" (Acts 4:32). Because of their shared love and fellowship with God, they believed and thought alike. Further, Paul writes that the church is actually "one body yet many members" (1 Cor. 12:12, 13), and therefore, "members of one another" (Eph. 4:25). The image is that of Jesus Christ being a head and all the church being His body, with every member of that body functioning under the direction and submission to the head. Certainly no body part acts independently! And so, every member of the body of Christ is to function together in subjection to the One who commands them.

---

[9] Jerry Bridges, *True Community: The Biblical Practice of Koinonia.* (Colorado Springs, CO: NavPress, 2012), 19.

However, as Christ's body, we do not function as automatons, carrying out rigid, mechanical deeds under the guise of "unity"—there is a greater purpose at work. In John 13, our Lord gives "a new commandment," which John later explains is not really a new command at all (1 John 2:7), but it is the command to "love one another, even as I have loved you, that you also love one another" (John 13:34). The absolute first responsibility of believers to Christ is to manifest love for each other. For what purpose? He continues, "By this all men will know that you are My disciples, if you have love for one another" (v. 35). So, there is a direct correlation between the shared love of all believers and their identification with Jesus Christ. To say it again, if we are to claim to belong to Christ, we must manifest a loving unity with other believers.

Sharing, Giving, and Serving

While it's one thing to use words like "love" and "unity," it is quite another thing to express those qualities practically and visibly. We are taught to manifest our love for others through our actions, namely through sharing, giving, and service. By our sharing and giving, we are "contributing to the needs of the saints" (Rom. 12:13), supplying for others' needs (see 2 Cor. 8:13-14), and thereby "doing good and sharing" (Heb. 13:16). As we have been specially gifted by God, we are to "employ it in serving one another, as good stewards of the manifold grace of God" (1 Pet. 4:10). We see this demonstrated beautifully in the first assembly, as the believers "had all things in common" (v. 44) and even "began selling their property and possessions, and were sharing them with all, as anyone might have need" (v. 45). On the nature of their sharing, James Boice writes,

> The early church shared their possessions, not because they were communists or socialists—not because they were forced to share their things—but for a far better reason. They shared their goods because they were generous, and they were generous because they had learned generosity from God. God had been generous with them. So because God had been generous with them, they were determined to be generous with one another.[10]

---

[10] James Montgomery Boice, *Acts: An Expositional Commentary*. (Grand Rapids, MI: Baker, 1997), 60.

More than simply bringing a plate of cookies to the church pot-luck (which is always appreciated by pastors!), true fellowship exists in the sharing of all aspects of life. It involves opening your heart, your home, your refrigerator, even your wallet. David Smith is right when he says "the essential basis of *koinōnia* rests upon an awareness of a common faith in Jesus Christ, a common experience of trans-formation, and a common hope of salvation, all of which issue in a common expression of Christian love."[11] While the church is to de-vote itself to fellowship—a shared life together—it must also mature through another means: discipleship.

Discipleship: Teaching Others to be like Christ

While it might seem like the solution for New Englanders' isolation-ism is simply to get together and socialize, there's a bit more to Chris-tian community than this. Sharing life together is essential, but it is only the beginning. Once believers are together and in fellowship, there is still more work to be done.

The Mandate for Discipleship

After His resurrection, and before ascending to heaven, the Lord Jesus imparted some final instructions to His followers. In what is known as The Great Commission, He says, "Go therefore and make disciples of all the nations, baptizing them in the name of the Fa-ther and the Son and the Holy Spirit, teaching them to observe all that I commanded you" (Matt. 28:19-20a). While the commission includes an element of being sent into all the world, the primary command is to *make disciples*.

A disciple is a learner, a pupil, a student, *"one who comes to be taught."*[12] Christ's desire was for the discipleship process He began with His followers to continue through them and beyond. Further, He instructs them to "[teach] them to observe all that I commanded you" (v. 20; cf. John 14:15, 15:14). The program of learning is to result in the obedience of the disciple to the commands of Christ. In the end, obedience to Christ results in "becoming conformed to

[11] Smith, *All God's People*, 345-346.

[12] J. Dwight Pentecost, *Design for Discipleship: Discovering God's Blueprint for the Christian Life*. (Grand Rapids, MI: Kregel, 1996), 10. Emphasis original.

the image of [God's] Son" (Rom. 8:29); in other words, we are to become like Christ (see Matt. 5:48; 1 Cor. 11:1; Eph. 5:1). How will this be done? Through modeling and imitation.

The Titus 2 Model

One of the clearest prescriptions for discipleship within a church context is laid out in Paul's letter to Titus. In chapter 2, Paul exhorts the young pastor to "speak the things which are fitting for sound doctrine" (v. 1). After setting the stage for orthodoxy, Paul lays out an all-inclusive plan for the church. He writes,

> *Older men* are to be temperate, dignified, sensible, sound in faith, in love, in perseverance.
>
> *Older women* likewise are to be reverent in their behavior, not malicious gossips, nor enslaved to much wine, teaching what is good, that they may encourage the young women...
>
> [*Young women are*] to love their husbands, to love their children, to be sensible, pure, workers at home, kind, being subject to their own husbands, that the word of God may not be dishonored.
>
> Likewise, urge the *young men* to be sensible; in all things show yourself to be an example of good deeds, with purity in doctrine, dignified, sound in speech which is beyond reproach, in order that the opponent may be put to shame, having nothing bad to say about us. (Titus 2:2-8, emphasis added)

In this short paragraph, Paul lists four basic categories of people within the church: older men, older women, younger women, and younger men. It's important to note that Paul is likely referring to Titus in verses 7 and 8, using him as an example for the other young men to follow. But the model is clear. The older men (v. 2) are to spend their time instructing the younger men (vv. 6-8), while the older women (v. 3) are to instruct the younger women (vv. 4-5).

We notice that Paul does not give any qualifiers here. He does not say, "Super-spiritual men should teach the younger men who are interested," nor does he say, "Make sure the older women have enough adult children so the young moms will believe she knows what she's talking about." Nothing like that! Rather, Paul points to the fact that *all* members of the church are valuable and have the responsibility to bring up the next generation. The problem arises when we think we need to farm out discipleship to someone "more qualified" or to a program inclusive enough to mass produce disciples. LeRoy Eims points out the error in this kind of thinking. He writes,

> The ministry is to be carried on by people, not programs. It is to be carried out by *someone* and not by some *thing*. Disciples cannot be mass produced. We cannot drop people into a 'program' and see disciples emerge at the end of the production line. It takes time to make disciples. It takes individual, personal attention. It takes hours of prayer for them. It takes patience and understanding to teach them how to get into the Word of God for themselves, how to feed and nourish their souls, and by the power of the Holy Spirit how to apply the word to their lives. And it takes being an example to them of all of the above.[13]

In the end, it will only be through the diligent efforts of godly saints that discipleship will be accomplished. So, what is to be the content of discipleship?

It's important to note that apart from the Word of God itself, the Bible makes no mandate for curriculum. But the essence of teaching others to obey Christ boils down to an approach that must include all aspects of their life. Genuine discipleship is teaching others how to live the Christian life (see 2 Tim. 2:2). LeRoy Eims again notes, "When you start spending individual time with another Christian for the purpose of having a ministry in his or her life—time together in the Word, prayer, fellowship, systematic training—something happens in your own life as well."[14] Not only are disciples grown and taught to obey Christ, but the bond between believers is strengthened.

---

[13] LeRoy Eims, *The Lost Art of Disciple Making*. (Grand Rapids, MI: Zondervan, 1978), 45-46. Emphases original.
[14] Ibid., 26.

One of the problems within Northeast churches is a lack of qualified leaders. There are a plethora of single-pastor churches where the burden of discipling the flock is placed squarely on the shoulders of one tired servant. But according to Ephesians 4:12, church leaders are given by God to the church "for the equipping of the saints for the work of service, to the building up of the body of Christ." Leaders are to train the saints so that they may get busy serving, discipling, and evangelizing. However, many New England congregations have completely missed this imperative. Commenting on this problem, Ray Stedman explains,

> Somehow, the church lost sight of the concept, so clearly stated in Ephesians 4, that all Christians are 'in the ministry.' The proper task of the four support ministries we have examined is to train, motivate, and strengthen the people—so called 'ordinary laypeople'—to do the work of ministry. When the ministry was left to the 'professionals,' there was nothing left for the people to do other than come to church and listen. They were told that it was their responsibility to bring the world into the church building to hear the pastor preach the gospel. Soon Christianity became little more than a Sunday-morning spectator sport, much like the definition of football: twenty-two men down on the field, desperately in need of rest, and twenty thousand in the grandstands, desperately in need of exercise.[15]

The church must not waffle on their God-given imperative to minister to one another. The pastors and church leaders exist primarily to provide the church with all the tools necessary to help them do it.

In the end, we know that, "As iron sharpens iron, so one man sharpens another" (Prov. 27:17). We are called to help each other grow into maturity, "to the measure of the stature which belongs to the fullness of Christ" (Eph. 4:13). Ultimately, as John MacArthur writes, "you're basically teaching him or her to pursue a godly lifestyle. You're teaching them biblical responses. A person is spiritually mature when his or her involuntary responses are godly. That's how you know if the Spirit of God has control in someone's life."[16]

---

[15] Ray C. Stedman, *Body Life*. (Grand Rapids, MI: Discovery House, 1972), 111-112.
[16] MacArthur, *The Master's Plan for the Church*, 68.

However, with every instructional step taken, there is often the need for correctional ones.

Counseling: Mending Hearts

In a perfect world, Christians would always and only be loving and building up one another. Every word would be an encouraging word, a positive word. But because we are living in a fallen world, and because our sinful natures plague us at every turn, we are not always afforded the luxury of such ease in ministry. Instead, people have problems. People get hurt. People hurt others. And *believers* are charged with the ministry of counseling.

In recent years, secular psychology has hijacked the discipline of counseling, and the church has been more than eager to export *problem solving* to the "experts." But this must not be! First and foremost, the fundamental issue has to do with the nature of sin. While secular counseling is all too quick to assign all psychological problems to outside factors, the Bible points to the root of much of our grief: our own fallen nature. These two belief systems are diametrically opposed to one another and any attempt to marry them leads only to confusion.

The second major problem with exporting counseling is that it robs the church of the responsibility—and the joy!—of caring for one another. In fact, we are to "[bear] one another's burdens and thus fulfill the law of Christ" (Gal. 6:2). The Bible teaches that the solution to life's problems is found in Jesus Christ, often mediated through the ministry of the local church. If we are to love one another as Christ loves us (John 13:34-45), then we will not shy away from a ministry of counseling.

A Biblical Approach

For a century, secular psychology and counseling were ruled by the theories and treatments of Sigmund Freud. But by the mid-1960s, the church began to rediscover biblical counseling. While the Lord moved mightily in many people, the greatest impact humanly-speaking was through the pioneering work of Jay E. Adams. In 1970, Adams published his groundbreaking book, *Competent to Counsel,* which put forth a system of counseling known as "Nouthetic Counseling"—a term coined by Adams. Derived from the Greek word *noutheteó*, which carries a variety of meanings, such as "admonish," "warn" and "teach,"[17] the concept of Nouthetic Counseling is relatively simple. In its most essential form, "Nouthetic confrontation, in its biblical usage, aims at straightening out the individual by changing his patterns of behavior to conform to biblical standards."[18] It is helping the believer to think and respond to their life's situations in the way the Bible teaches. While there is certainly a place for pastors and Christian counselors to administer such counseling, Adams is adamant that true biblical counseling is "a work in which all of God's people may participate."[19]

The Bible itself is crystal clear in its commands to believers that we must "admonish one another" (Rom. 15:14; Col. 1:28; 3:16), "encourage one another" (Heb. 3:13), "comfort one another" (1 Thes. 4:18), "build up one another" (1 Thes. 5:11), "confess your sins to one another" (Jas. 5:16), and bear with one another (Rom. 15:1; 1 Cor. 13:7; Gal. 6:1-2). The responsibility to care for one another in the midst of difficulty does not only fall to "professionals" but to each and every member of the body of Christ. While each situation is different, it's helpful to look briefly at the types of trouble individuals fall into.

Three Areas of Trouble

While it's impossible to simplify all human problems into nice, neat categories, let me suggest three main areas of trouble that must be tended to by the church.

First, in the event of *calamity*. From a human perspective, this is sheer tragedy. Anything from losing a home or a job, to the untimely death of a loved one. A sudden diagnosis of a deadly disease or a disfiguring accident falls into this category of calamity. It is times like these when a person needs comfort and counsel from the brethren. When tragedy strikes, the church must go on high alert and minister to those in trouble, reminding them of God's goodness, kindness, and sovereignty (see Job 38:1-42:6). But in the midst of deepest

---

[17] Jay E. Adams, *Competent to Counsel: Introduction to Nouthetic Counseling.* (Grand Rapids, MI: Zondervan, 1970), 44.

[18] Ibid., 46.

[19] Ibid., 42.

darkness, the church must be willing and prepared to care for their own as they would for themselves (Matt. 22:39). This requires empathy. Conversely, Jerry Bridges notes, "The reason we don't experience this family-like empathy with our suffering brothers and sisters in Christ is that we have not yet been fully gripped by the truth that we are in a community relationship with them."[20] We must remember that we are members of one another; we are one body in Christ (Rom. 12:5; Eph. 4:25).

Second, in the suffering of *wounds by others*. There are times when a person is hurt by others without provocation. In fact, the Lord told the disciples that this is inevitable (John 15:18-21; 16:1-4; cf. 1 Pet. 4:12-19). While being wounded by others may come through no fault of our own, our response must be godly. The temptation is to respond sinfully, returning scorn on those who have hurt us. But through the encouragement and admonition of faithful believers, we must be taught to respond without sinning (Rom. 12:14, 17-19; Eph. 4:26). Not only must we be counseled to respond biblically, we also need to be lifted up, knowing that we can suffer well and bring glory to Jesus Christ in doing so (Matt. 5:10-12; 1 Pet. 2:21; 4:1).

Third, in the *committing of sin*. Perhaps the most critical need whereby Nouthetic counseling must be administered is in the area of sin. The most loving thing a believer can do for another is confront them about their sin and encourage them to repent. James teaches, "If any among you strays from the truth, and one turns him back, let him know that he who turns a sinner from the error of his way will save his soul from death, and will cover a multitude of sins" (5:19-20; cf. 1 Pet. 4:8). Further, faithful believers are to help restore sinning brothers "in a spirit of gentleness" (Gal. 6:1). What happens when a sinning brother becomes caught in sin? We will explore this issue in the next section.

Discipline: Purifying the Church

Teaching His disciples, Jesus said, "For the Son of Man came to seek and to save the lost" (Luke 19:10; cf. Matt. 18:11). His desire is not

---

[20] Bridges, *True Community*, 133.

for the lost to perish, but come to saving faith. However, sin causes the believer to stumble and places them out of communion with God, and it can shipwreck their faith (cf. 1 Tim. 1:19). In Matthew 18, Jesus instructs the church to become an instrument through which believers can be steered away from sin and back to God.

> If your brother sins against you, go and tell him his fault, between you and him alone. If he listens to you, you have gained your brother. But if he does not listen, take one or two others along with you, that every charge may be established by the evidence of two or three witnesses. If he refuses to listen to them, tell it to the church. And if he refuses to listen even to the church, let him be to you as a Gentile and a tax collector. (Matt. 18:15-17)

This passage is famously known as the "church discipline" passage, but in reality, it's more of the "How to rescue and restore believers" passage. R.T. France notes that "this is how a disciple is to act when he or she is aware that a fellow disciple is in spiritual danger, through sin."[21] Jesus presents four steps, each one increasing in intensity. But it's important to note that "we should try to keep the circle of people involved in a conflict *as small as possible for as long as possible.*"[22] John MacArthur writes, "The goal of church discipline is not to throw people out, embarrass them, be self-righteous, play God, or exercise authority and power in some unbiblical manner. The purpose of discipline is to bring people back into a pure relationship with God and with others in the assembly."[23] The ultimate goal is restoration; the motivation is love (1 Cor. 5:5).

Sadly, Matthew 18 has been abused. In some circles, it has been used as a proof text for witch-hunts and excommunication. Others have bypassed the first two steps and brought sinning members directly to the assembly for rebuke. However, this is *not* the spirit of Matthew 18! The heart of the command is to chasten and admonish sinning members privately with the goal of repentance and restoration.

---

[21] R.T. France, *The Gospel of Matthew.* NICNT (Grand Rapids, MI: Eerdmans, 2007), 690.

[22] Ken Sande, *The Peacemaker: A Biblical Guide to Resolving Personal Conflict.* (Grand Rapids, MI: Baker Books, 1991), 186. Emphasis included.

[23] MacArthur, *The Master's Plan for the Church,* 267.

When the first two steps are minimized or ignored, it gives the transgression even more space to grow into an oak tree of sinfulness. By the time the sin is made public, it's often too late. I wonder how much gross sin could be weeded out at the heart level if faithful believers would simply go to their brothers and sisters in a humble truthfulness.

The real function of the body of Christ here is to practice the discipline of *noutheteó*—admonishing, rebuking, instructing, and correcting. It is inter-personal. It is private. It is loving. We want to win over our sinning brothers and sisters, not force them out. With a pastoral heart, Ray Stedman writes, "Our goal as Christians should not be to go on a search-and-destroy mission against all the tares in the church, but to do everything we can to make the true wheat in the church so strong and healthy that the tares are powerless to damage it."[24]

We want to win over our brothers, but we must do it God's way, and that means we don't simply overlook or ignore sin. There will not be a revival of the Spirit without a revival of repentance and restoration. A lazy church that is unwilling to correct and chasten its members is a church that is destined to have its lampstand removed (cf. Rev. 2:5). We must be brave and loving enough to be honest with one another. There is a wicked myth that says staying silent somehow keeps the peace, thus maintaining unity. But we must be reminded that "obedience to Christ and his Word is more important than an artificial 'unity' built on disobedience and compromise."[25] We must be willing to abide in Christ and obey His precepts. The Bible teaches, "Faithful are the wounds of a friend" (Prov. 27:6) and those who seek the good of other believers act faithfully, demonstrating their obedience to the Great Commandment (Matt. 22:37-40).

The Lord Jesus Christ cares about the purity of His church, and He has charged us with the task of maintaining unity through loving confrontation. The false mind-your-own-business ethic that believes the confrontation over sin is "meddlesome" is wrong. Conversely, we are not to be "the sin police," digging up the sinful secrets of others. Instead, churches must commit themselves to addressing problems of sin in biblical ways.

---

[24] Stedman, *Body Life*, 17.
[25] Daniel E. Wray, *Biblical Church Discipline*. (Edinburgh: Banner of Truth, 1978), 10-11.

The Need for True Fellowship

In a time when New Englanders have grown cold toward one another, we must fight this cultural stronghold and work hard to build true community. The blessing of such fellowship is unique to the church; it is something the unbelieving world has never seen because the basis for love and unity within the body of Christ is found in Christ Himself. We are to extend grace and mercy, but also be the recipients of it. In order to foster a culture of community, we must build fellowship with one another, make disciples who will love and obey the Lord, counsel and admonish one another to live and act biblically, and deal with sin with a view to winning wandering souls back to God. In a region of closed-off people who tend to hide behind their fences, we must work to tear those fences down.

5

REDISCOVERING THE PATH

"Go therefore and make disciples of all the nations,
baptizing them in the name of the Father
and the Son and the Holy Spirit,
teaching them to observe all that I have commanded you;
and lo, I am with you always, even to the end of the age."

Matthew 28:19-20, NASB

Much of New England is rural and wooded, with miles and miles of hiking trails snaking through the forest green. One day, we took our family down one of these trails, following the markers as we went. After half an hour, however, we realized that the path was not so clear, and that we were off the trail. We needed to backtrack and find one of the orange markers. After retracing our steps, we were able to find the well-worn path and continue on to our destination. This is not unlike what has taken place in New England churches over the last century or so. In many cases, we have lost our way and found ourselves in unfamiliar territory. We need desperately to retrace our steps, and rediscover the path that God has set for us. Otherwise, we will find ourselves lost in the wilderness.

The Wrong Mission

Perhaps the most famous of Robert Frost's work is his poem, "The Road Not Taken," which romanticizes the journey down an untraveled path which leads to adventure. The poem is a rally cry for non-conformity and self-discovery, but this is not the ethic we should be chasing in the church. Why? Because God has defined our path; it's not a mystery. And He is calling us to obedience and faithfulness, not to reinventing the wheel. In a cultural landscape that overvalues relevance and innovation, while decrying time-test-ed methods and ideas, the ancient truths of Scripture have never been more discarded.

Churches in the Northeast have fallen victim to the absolute worst distractions away from biblical faithfulness, as we foolishly try and move the goal markers to suit our own fancy. In some churches, the highest priority has become *traditionalism*. They romanticize "the good ol' days" and reject any change, even if it's a correction toward biblical faithfulness. While godly tradition can be a blessed thing, it is not the *only* thing. Too often, we nullify the Word of God for the sake of our traditions.

In that same vein, many churches fall victim to *archealotry*—the worship of buildings. Churches have split over carpet shades and sanctuary decorations, over a common room, or even over a single treasured item. The oldest churches in America reside in the Northeast, and some church groups sacrifice everything simply to keep up their building, cutting off their nose to spite their face. Many church groups have forsaken all godliness and Christian witness in order to set up an idol—a pretty, white building with a proud steeple.

Scores of churches have wandered away from the Bible and thus from Christian orthodoxy, and have embraced *false doctrine*. Unitarianism (the rejection of the Trinity) and Universalism (the belief in universal salvation regardless of repentance and faith) have crippled whole denominations. Along with those major heresies, more subtle errors have crept in as well. In many cases, liberalism has created a hodge-podge of religious practices (called *syncretism*) in the interest of appearing "diverse" or "cultured."

However, the biggest departure from biblical orthodoxy has been the aggressive propagation of the *social gospel*. Popularized in the early twentieth century, the crux of the social gospel is the belief that churches exist to bring about the material welfare of whole communities. While it is theoretically built on the biblical concept of "love your neighbor" (Matt. 22:39), it does not ultimately lead to a saving relationship with Jesus Christ. This form of "love" has become an end unto itself; a generic sort of kindness that seeks to minister to felt needs, but with no intention of meeting people's greatest need—to be saved.

In the end, "doing good" or "making a difference" is a lost cause because it does not communicate the saving message of the gospel. In fact, it does not communicate any particular message at all, except that "we're here to give you things." Now, don't get me wrong, we are charged with the task of caring for the needs of others (Matt. 25:35-46; Rom. 12:13; Titus 2:14, 3:8, 14; Heb. 13:2; 1 Pet. 4:9), but it is always unto the Lord. Even Jesus Himself never divorced the meal from the message; caring for people was always tied to the good news of salvation. And when we spend all of our time focused on our traditions, our buildings, or good deeds, yet neglect our message, we have surely wandered off the path.

We must remind ourselves of our mission.

Our Mission

In the last chapter, we saw how the *identity* of the church is directly tied to that of Jesus Christ. However, it is more than simply an identification with Christ, but a deep and devoted love for Him which manifests itself through a shared love for the church. Once we know who we *are*, we must then determine what to *do*. What are the church's marching orders? Let's explore five common elements of the church's mission as they are seen throughout Scripture.

Preaching the Gospel

The first aspect of mission is evangelism through the explicit preaching of the gospel. Mark Dever notes, "The local church is God's evangelism plan."[1] While some have rightly distinguished between "evangelism" (witnessing in a local context) and "missions" (witnessing abroad),[2] for the sake of simplicity, I want to focus in on the task of evangelism itself. While it has been noted that "there are two ways to evangelize: through our lives and through our words,"[3] it must be said that there is a lack of gospel focus in New England. Far too many believers are unsure, unconvinced, and untrained when it comes to sharing the gospel message. Further, many lifelong

---

[1] Mark Dever, *Nine Marks of a Healthy Church*. (Wheaton, IL: Crossway, 2004), 15.
[2] Though I have seen this distinction made in several places, John MacArthur shares a helpful sentiment: "Missions is a worldwide view of evangelism." *The Master's Plan for the Church*. (Chicago, IL: Moody, 2008), 63.
[3] Ibid., 62.

churchgoers have never actually heard or believed a saving gospel, and therefore exist as tares in the Lord's wheat field. However, if we believe Scripture to be true, we must affirm that "the gospel is the power of God for salvation to everyone who believes" (Rom. 1:16) and unbelievers will never come to faith in Jesus Christ unless it is proclaimed (Rom. 10:14-17).

The word "gospel" (*euangelion*) means "good news"—specifically the good news of the finished, saving work of Jesus Christ. Further, to "evangelize" (*euangelizo*) is to proclaim that good news to others. While the gospel itself is a definite message with exact parts, the church's mission of evangelism is the act of sharing that message. Now, at this point, it must be said that there is a difference between sharing *the gospel* and sharing *your testimony*. While sharing the gospel consists of delivering the message of Christ, sharing testimony gives the effect of the gospel on us. Will Metzger notes,

> The content of our message is Christ and God, not our journey to faith. Our personal testimony may be included, but witnessing is more than reciting our spiritual autobiography. Specific truths about a specific person are the subject of our proclamation. A message has been committed to us—a word of reconciliation to the world (2 Cor 5:19).[4]

During the Olivet Discourse, Jesus told His disciples that "The gospel of the kingdom shall be preached in the whole world as a testimony to all the nations" (Matt. 24:14). This work of gospel-preaching would begin during the ministry of Christ (Matt. 4:23; Mark 1:14-15) and continue all the way to the end of days. More specifically, Jesus later said, "Thus it is written, that the Christ would suffer and rise again from the dead the third day, and that repentance for forgiveness of sins would be proclaimed in His name to all the nations" (Luke 24:46-47). Elsewhere, the command is given to "Go into all the world and preach the gospel to all creation" (Mark 16:15).

The apostle Paul understood the mandate for gospel preaching. He reminded the Corinthian church that the gospel truths of

---

[4] Will Metzger, *Tell the Truth: The Whole Gospel to the Whole Person by Whole People.* (Downers Grove, IL: InterVarsity, 2002), 27.

Christ's death, burial, and resurrection were of "first importance" (1 Cor. 15:3-4). In fact, the gospel was so important, he had declared to them, "For I determined to know nothing among you except Jesus Christ, and Him crucified" (1 Cor. 2:2). By all means, Paul did not undervalue the rest of the Scriptures—he declared "the whole counsel of God" in Ephesus (Acts 20:27, ESV)—but in light of the dire importance of the gospel, Paul kept it foremost in his mind.

While it must be said that it is necessary for Christians to "live out their faith" by being above reproach in character, the gospel message does not simply get absorbed by others through osmosis. The message must be explicit.[5] We must tell unbelievers that they have violated God's perfect law, committed sinful rebellion against Him, and are destined for eternal conscious punishment—hell. However, because of God's grace, love, and mercy, He sent His Son into the world—the person of Jesus Christ, who is Himself fully God and fully man—to give Himself as a substitute sacrifice for our sin. On the cross, Jesus bore our sins on His body, suffered and satisfied the full fury of God's wrath, secured the forgiveness of sins, and restored the possibility of relationship with the Father. And then, on the third day, Jesus rose from the grave to bring new life to all who repent of their sins and trust in Him for salvation.

We cannot skimp on this message; a whole region full of lost souls are at stake. We must preach, explain, and share the gospel.

Making Disciples

While gospel preaching is certainly the tip of the spear, it is not ultimately the end of our mission. Before ascending to heaven, the Lord Jesus Christ left the disciples with their marching orders. We read:

> And Jesus came up and spoke to them, saying, 'All authority has been given to Me in heaven and on earth. Go therefore and make disciples of all the nations, baptizing them in the name of the Father and the Son and the Holy Spirit, teaching them to observe all that I have commanded you; and lo, I am with you always, even to the end of the age.' (Matt. 28:18-20)

---

[5] A helpful book on this topic is Matt Chandler with Jared Wilson, *The Explicit Gospel*. Wheaton, IL: Crossway, 2014.

Much has been written about this passage, aptly referred to as "The Great Commission." While the mantra of many churches through the years has been an emphasis on the command to "Go!" a closer look yields a different perspective. New Testament scholar D.A. Carson notes, "In the Greek, 'go'—like 'baptizing' and 'teaching'—is a participle. Only the verb 'make disciples' is imperative."[6] So, the real focus is less on "going" and more on disciple-making. As we saw previously, a "disciple" is a student, and in this context, it is a Christian who is learning to obey the Lord Jesus Christ. And so, the primary mission of Christian believers is to win and teach Christian believers.

This command flies in the face of the modern demand for "decisions"—a comparatively recent evangelical trend born out of the Revivalism era. Since the Second Great Awakening, and certainly since the Billy Graham Crusades of the 1950s and 1960s, we have been hyper-focused on obtaining professions of faith, winning converts rather than disciples. After all, it's more exciting to report large numbers of new believers who come to Christ all at once than it is to track with a smaller number of growing disciples. But we need a radical shift in mindset away from decision-based interaction and toward long-term discipleship. We need to maintain a long view of ministry with our people. Otherwise, we'll end up with a church full of one-year-old Christians twenty times over.

Without restating everything mentioned in the previous chapter, it is important to note that true discipleship is an involved ministry. It is relational, not transactional. While Scripture doesn't give a prescribed method or an official curriculum, we do have the basic parameters given to us by the Lord Himself. In looking again at Matthew 28:20, we read that we are to be "teaching them to observe all that I have commanded you." A closer examination reveals that the primary aspect of discipleship is *teaching*. While this might not always take the form of didactic classroom-style teaching, it certainly may include elements of it. We must become devoted to teaching disciples in any way that information can be successfully received and rightly applied.

[6] D.A. Carson, "Matthew" in *The Expositor's Bible Commentary: Volume 8*. (Grand Rapids, MI: Zondervan, 1984), 595.

Further, this teaching and learning is not to stop at the head, rather, it is to be done with a view to *obedience*. The Lord's command to "teach… them to obey" contains the imperative of application. What we *learn* about Jesus must directly inform how we *live* for Jesus. After all, we are exhorted to "prove [ourselves to be] doers of the word, and not merely hearers who delude themselves" (Jas. 1:22). Hearing and learning must always be with a view to doing.

Finally, the Lord specifies the amount of content to be taught; "teaching them to obey *all* that I have commanded." While some may be content with exhausting Jesus' teachings in the Gospels only, we must remember that the whole canon of Scripture is to be learned and obeyed (cf. 2 Tim. 3:16-17). Certainly, a healthy discipleship process should include comprehensive Bible knowledge, as well as theology (biblical doctrine). Again, none of this content can be learned in a bubble; it must be implanted in order that it might bear the fruit of righteousness in the disciple.

Bearing Witness to Christ

A third aspect of the church's mission has to do with our witness. In His parting words to the disciples in Acts 1:8, the Lord Jesus told them, "But you will receive power when the Holy Spirit comes upon you; and you shall be My witnesses both in Jerusalem, and in all Judea and Samaria, and even to the remotest part of the earth." The fulfillment of their spiritual empowerment came at Pentecost (Acts 2:1-13), but the remainder of their ministry (and ours) would consist of bearing witness to Christ.

We get our word "martyr" from the Greek word *martyría* which means "witness" or "testimony." The early disciples were first-hand witnesses to the life, sufferings, death, and resurrection of Jesus (Luke 24:46-48; John 15:26-27; Acts 2:32; 1 John 1:1-4). It is by their testimony that we believe the truth of the gospel. But even now, we are to function as witnesses to the person and work of Jesus Christ, and to the divine miracle of salvation and sanctification. DeYoung and Gilbert write, "The Bible teaches that we Christians are to be a people of both declaration and demonstration."[7] In other words, we are witnesses through *what we say* and *what we do*.

---

[7] Kevin DeYoung & Greg Gilbert, *What Is the Mission of the Church? Making Sense of Social Justice, Shalom, and the Great Commission.* (Wheaton, IL: Crossway, 2011.), 223.

While we are certainly called to bear witness to Christ with our whole lives, there are elements worth noting. First, our *profession*. This is the outward declaration of gospel truth and the affirmation of its saving power. Speaking with unbridled zeal, Paul boldly declared, "For I am not ashamed of the gospel, for it is the power of God for salvation to everyone who believes" (Rom. 1:16). Not only was he unashamed of the boldness of the gospel, he was unapologetic of its message. We must grasp the same tenacity in our profession of such a gospel, for it has the ability to tear down strongholds and bring the spiritually dead to life.

Second, our *testimony*. While we are to bear witness to the gospel itself, we also maintain our own personal witness to what the gospel has done in us. This is our story; our testimony of the grace of God in our lives. We remember our lost, blind, and wretched condition before Christ, and how we have been regenerated, forgiven, redeemed, and saved, being sanctified daily. Our testimonies give powerful evidence that God is still intimately involved with this world to the praise of His own glorious grace—our testimonies, after all, are our modern day stories of how God has intervened and saved us.

Third, our *love*. In the Upper Room discourse, Jesus stressed the importance of love between believers. He said, "A new commandment I give to you, that you love one another, even as I have loved you, that you also love one another. By this all men will know that you are My disciples, if you have love for one another" (John 13:34-35). While there is an intrinsic value to Christian love—it fulfills the Great Commandment (Matt. 22:36-40)—in the context of Christ's command, there is an element of witness. By demonstrating Christ-like love for other believers, we bear witness to the truth of the gospel and identify ourselves as His disciples.

Fourth, our *deeds*. Paul's reoccurring exhortation to the believers on Crete was that they would "be careful to engage in good deeds" (Titus 3:8, 14). In fact, he reaffirms that Christ Jesus has redeemed and purified the church for Himself, in order that we might be "zealous for good deeds" (2:14). Ultimately, not only will devotion to good conduct stifle dishonor (2:5) and slander (2:8), but it will prove to make the gospel attractive to non-believers (2:10). In the end, Jesus affirmed that good deeds are to result in the true worship of God—"Let your light shine before men in such a way that they may see your good works, and glorify your Father who is in heaven" (Matt. 5:16).

For two thousand years, the church has borne witness to Christ, in order that He might be glorified and the lost might be saved. But our witness isn't simply to win someone over to "a better life" or "a sense of belonging;" we are bearing witness to the person and work of Jesus Christ. Michael Horton writes, "The early Christians were not fed to wild beasts or dipped in wax and set ablaze as lamps in Nero's garden because they thought Jesus was a helpful coach or role model but because they witnessed to him as the only Lord and Savior of the world."[8]

Being Sanctified and Matured

A fourth aspect of the church's mission surrounds the character of individual believers. While this may seem out of place, since it does not seem to fit the category of "active" mission, the church is no less required to grow in likeness to Jesus Christ as she does the work of ministry. Even from the outset, the church was chosen by God in Christ to "be holy and blameless before Him" (Eph. 1:4; 5:27). In fact, the ultimate end of this calling is unto Christlikeness. "For whom He foreknew, He also predestined to become conformed to the image of His Son" (Rom. 8:29).

In Paul's letter to the Ephesians, he points to the maturity and unity of the body as a result of fruitful ministry (Eph. 4:12-16). Our natural tendency is to place evangelism up on a pedestal twenty miles above every other Christian endeavor. It's not that evangelism isn't vital, rather, it is the healthy fruit of a sanctified heart. In another place, Paul wrote, "For this is the will of God, your sanctification" (1 Thes. 4:3). While it must be said that effective evangelism and ministry *can* be accomplished by those with unsanctified, selfish motives (Phil. 1:15-18), it is not ultimately preferable. God's desire is for His people to be holy (Lev. 11:44, 19:2, 20:7; Matt. 5:48; 1 Pet. 1:16).

But is this truly the mission of the church? Does it really reflect God's desired ministry for His people? I believe it does. When we

---

[8] Michael Horton, *The Gospel Commission: Recovering God's Strategy for Making Disciples.* (Grand Rapids, MI: Baker, 2011) 32-33.

weigh out these two endeavors—evangelism and sanctification—it's important to see that they are not mutually exclusive. If the heart is the origin of the fruit of our lives (Prov. 4:23; Matt. 15:19; Luke 6:45), then faithfully-executed ministry must find its origin in a sanctified life. Surely the church would not desire to be like the Cretans who profess to know God, but deny Him by their deeds (Titus 1:16)!

I fear that the Christian mission has been largely compromised because of hypocrisy within the church. We have devalued holiness and, in many cases, made provision for sin. While a large number of professing Christians in New England have veered away from the biblical mandate to preach the gospel and make disciples, there still remain gospel-focused congregations, yet many of them have invalidated their gospel and witness by their ungodly conduct. Sadly, the "well, at least we've got the message right" excuse will not negate the absence of holiness and righteousness.

We must see that devotion to spiritual growth and maturity will bear the fruit of evangelism and discipleship. After all, Spirit-filled believers are Spirit-willed believers—a people that desire the things that God desires (Ps. 37:4; Rom. 12:2). A heart that is transformed by and transfixed on the things of God cannot keep silent! But let us devote ourselves to godliness, lest we ruin our testimony. And let's heed these fearful words:

> Great damage has been done to the cause of Christ by unhealthy saints who attempted to carry out evangelistic or social ministry with great zeal but without true spiritual health. Burdened with unsolved problems in their own lives, often displaying unhealthy (and unrecognized) hypocrisy and prejudice, these Christians bring the body of Christ and the gospel of Christ into disrepute in the world. Their worship has become a dull, lifeless, predictable ritual. They display more reverence for [their] own religious traditions than for biblical truth. They talk about superficial matters around the coffeepot after church, and they call it 'fellowship' and 'Christian love'—even though there is little if any real involvement in each others' lives.[9]

---

[9] Ray Stedman, *Body Life*. (Grand Rapids, MI: Discovery House, 1972), 146.

Glorifying God

The Westminster Shorter Catechism (1647) famously states that "Man's chief end is to glorify God, and to enjoy him forever" (derived from Ps. 86; Isa. 60:21; Rom. 11:36; 1 Cor. 6:20, 10:31; Rev. 4:11; etc.). While this seems straight-forward, we would do well to unpack this concept a bit further.

First, what is God's *glory*? In Exodus 33, Moses asks the Lord to show him His glory. After placing Moses in the cleft of a rock and covering him in order to protect him (Ex. 33:22), God passes by Moses and displays His glory. While he is able to glance at the majestic brilliance of God's visible glory, Moses also witnesses the Lord's proclamation: "The Lord, the Lord God, compassionate and gracious, slow to anger, and abounding in lovingkindness and truth; who keeps lovingkindness for thousands, who forgives iniquity, transgression and sin; yet He will by no means leave the guilty unpunished, visiting the iniquity of fathers on the children and on the grandchildren to the third and fourth generation" (Ex. 34:6-7). In conjunction with displaying His radiant visible glory, God also declared a multitude of His own attributes—His character. In defining it, John Piper notes, "The term *glory of God* in the Bible generally refers to the visible splendor or moral beauty of God's manifold perfections."[10] On its two-sided nature, Herman Bavinck writes, "God's glory indicates the splendor and brilliancy that is inseparably connected with all of God's virtues and with his self-revelation in nature and grace."[11] In short, it is the sum of all God's brilliance and attributes.

Now, we must answer a second question: what does it mean to *glorify God*? It must be said that God cannot be given what He already possesses. No man gives God anything, and certainly not His own glory. So, to glorify God is not to add to or strengthen His glory. However, we can ascribe glory to God; we can affirm His glorious nature and worship Him rightly. In Psalm 29, worshipers are exhorted to "Ascribe to the Lord, O sons of the mighty, ascribe to the Lord glory and strength. Ascribe to the Lord the glory due to His name; worship the

---

[10] John Piper, *Desiring God: Meditations of a Christian Hedonist.* (Colorado Springs, CO: Multnomah, 1986), 308. Emphasis original.

[11] Herman Bavinck, *The Doctrine of God.* Translated, Edited and Outlined by William Hendriksen. (Edinburgh: Banner of Truth, 1977), 248.

Lord in holy array" (vv. 1-2). Ultimately, every creature on earth was created to give/ascribe glory to God (Ps. 150:6).

In fact, in the beginning, God created humankind "in His image" to be like Him and share in a small sliver of His glory. Piper beautifully illustrates, "We were made to be prisms refracting the light of God's glory into all of life."[12] While this command to glorify God falls to every person, not every person obeys. And so, it is the church's role to sound a trumpet for all to hear: "Worship the Lord and give Him glory!"

When a person is born again, saved by the grace of God, it is done "to the praise of His glory" (Eph. 1:6, 12, 14). Once we are in Him, we are to "do all to the glory of God" (1 Cor. 10:31). In other words, everything we do must be in view of the honor, worship, and adoration of God. We are to worship God with our bodies (1 Cor. 6:20) as well as with our minds (Rom. 12:1-2). This essential mandate does not bypass a single area of life.

How do we glorify God? Piper writes,

If God made us for His glory, it is clear that we should live for His glory. Our duty comes from God's design. What does it mean to glorify God? It does not mean that we make Him more glorious. It means to acknowledge His glory, to value it above all things, and to make it known.[13]

And if all humans were ultimately created to live for His glory, certainly the church must make this their chief end. This includes glorifying God through all matters of life and ministry, sharing the gospel and being transformed by it. If we reduce the Great Commission to merely a punchlist of religious tasks, we have missed the mark completely. Our underlying motive must be to make much of God and adore Him supremely. This is the end of all we do: to know God and make Him known. Mark Dever aptly states,

The church ultimately exists for the glory of God. Whether pursuing missions or evangelism; edifying one another through prayer and Bible study; encouraging growth in ho-

---

[12] Piper, *Desiring God*, 56.
[13] Ibid.

liness; or assembling for public praise, prayer, and instruction, this one purpose prevails.[14]

Retracing Our Steps

The church cannot afford to miss the mark when it comes to our mission. Lives literally hang in the balance! If we are to hold on to any hope of true spiritual revival in New England, we need to make sure that we are aiming at the right target, and traveling down the right path.

We cannot be focused on self-preservation, whether it be our traditionalism or our buildings. We cannot be focused on simply meeting felt needs to no end, engaging in a social gospel. Instead, we must keep our focus on the commands of Jesus Christ, who Himself is "the author and perfecter of faith" (Heb. 12:2). We must humbly confess that He knows what is best for church, as the church belongs to Him. The Lord sets the agenda and commands us to follow His plan.

We must be committed to all aspects of the Great Commission, explicit *and* implicit. We must take great care to share the gospel, calling people to repentance and faith. We must make disciples, teaching believers to obey all that the Lord commands. We must bear witness to Christ through our words, our lives, and our love. We must devote ourselves to sanctification, growing to be more like Christ. And our motive must be to put the glory of God on display, ascribing to Him the highest honor and praise. Restated another way, Kevin DeYoung and Greg Gilbert arrive at a conclusive statement:

> The Mission of the church is to go into the world and make disciples by declaring the gospel of Jesus Christ in the power of the Holy Spirit and gathering these disciples into churches, that they might worship the Lord and obey his commands now and in eternity to the glory of God the Father.[15]

But, how do we know where we are with this? We know that New England is hurting, with many churches struggling to stay afloat. How do we self-assess and put these things into practice? How

---

[14] Mark Dever, *The Church: The Gospel Made Visible.* (Nashville, TN: B&H, 2012), 77.
[15] DeYoung & Gilbert, *What Is the Mission of the Church?*, 62. Emphasis original.

do we match our zeal with our actions? Because if we do not become doers of the word, but hearers only, we will delude ourselves and doom ourselves to a worse fate. How do we get the train moving? That's what we're going to talk about next.

6

REIGNITING THE LAMPS

"Remember therefore from where you have fallen,
and repent and do the deeds you did at first;
or else I am coming to you, and will remove
your lampstand out of its place – unless you repent."

Rev. 2:5, NAS

In the olden days, city streetlamps had to be lit by hand, as a workman would pace up and down with a pole in his hand, igniting the wicks. In strong storms, however, those lamps were prone to go out. That is what has happened to churches in the Northeast. The hurricane winds of liberalism have blown out the lamps in many of the churches. Further, the remaining churches are still under attack, their flames flickering, and they must heed the warnings of the Lord Jesus Christ or else they too will be extinguished.

The Church Who Lost Their Love

Contrary to popular belief, the book of Revelation isn't all dragons, diadems, and destruction. The opening chapters contain exhortation and instruction for the churches of the first century. Chapters 2 and 3 address seven main churches in Asia Minor. Each of them need various prescriptions from the Lord. But it is the church at Ephesus that piques our interest.

We read:

To the angel of the church in Ephesus write: The One who holds the seven stars in His right hand, the One who walks among the seven golden lampstands, says this: 'I know your deeds and your toil and perseverance, and that you cannot tolerate evil men, and you put to the test those who call themselves apostles, and they are not, and you found them to be false; and you have perseverance and have endured for My name's sake, and have not grown weary. But I have this against you, that you have left your first love. Therefore remember from where you have fallen, and repent and do the deeds you did at first; or else I am coming to you and will remove your lampstand out of its place—unless you repent. Yet this you do have, that you hate the deeds of the Nicolaitans, which I also hate. He who has an ear, let him hear what the Spirit says to the churches. To him who overcomes, I will grant to eat of the tree of life which is in the Paradise of God.' (Revelation 2:1-7)

The city of Ephesus was one of the major religious centers in the known world. It housed the temple of the fertility goddess, Artemis. In the midst of a vastly pagan culture, the Ephesian church held the line. By all rights, they had begun well; they were a faithful church. The Lord praises them for their strengths in verses 2 and 3, noting their "deeds and [their] toil and perseverance" (v. 2). He even makes note of their love for the truth manifested in their hatred for false teaching (v. 2, 6). According to all outward markers, they were a good church.

However, the Lord rebukes them in verse 4 for one fundamental flaw: they've lost their first love. This is a serious problem that endangers their very existence. In fact, it's so bad that if not remedied, will lead to their utter destruction. Scholars don't agree on whether their love-loss is referring to Christ or to one another, but commentator Robert Mounce notes, "A cooling of personal love for God inevitably results in the loss of harmonious relationships within the body of believers."[1]

The believers at Ephesus had become so zealous for defending the truth of God, they forgot to love the God of the truth. Simon Kistemaker notes, "the church that Jesus addressed no longer consisted of first-generation believers but of second- and third-generation Christians. These people lacked the enthusiasm their parents and grandparents demonstrated. They functioned not as propagators of the faith

---

[1] Robert H. Mounce, *The Book of Revelation*. (Grand Rapids, MI: Eerdmans, 1997), 70.

but as caretakers and custodians."[2] When the mantle was passed to them from their parents, genuine love was not passed on with it.

The Lord warns the Ephesian church that if they do not reignite their love, He will remove their lampstand (v. 5). It's important to note that, while the individual believers will not lose their salvation, the church will lose its ability to bear witness to those around it. We know from history that the Ephesians were never able to repair the damage. In fact, this abandonment of Christ's love was so catastrophic that it "opened the doors to spiritual apathy, indifference to others, love for the world, compromise with evil, judgment, and ultimately, the death of the church altogether."[3]

The lesson to be learned here is that "Good works and pure doctrine are not adequate substitutes for that rich relationship of mutual love shared by those who have experienced for the first time the redemptive love of God."[4] If our actions are devoid of a true love for God, then they are worthless (Titus 1:16). Further, the danger is that "we can become so occupied with doing *for* Christ as to miss becoming *like* Christ."[5] When our love for the Lord declines, the soul drifts away from Him. We hear so much these days about the danger of "mission drift" but the greater danger is that of "soul drift."[6]

This is the problem with the churches in New England—we've lost our first love. Our parents and grandparents fled to these shores to establish faithful churches. They stirred up godly affections for Christ and set the world aflame with the gospel. They built seminaries and sent missionaries. They were a light to all the nations. But like the Ephesians in Revelation 2, we have inherited their faith without inheriting their love. Maybe we haven't completely lost the gospel, but our light is so dim, one strong gust of apostasy would extinguish our light forever. O Lord, may this never be! What must be done?

---

[2] Simon J. Kistemaker, *New Testament Commentary: Exposition of the Book of Revelation.* (Grand Rapids, MI: Baker, 2001), 115.

[3] John MacArthur, *The MacArthur New Testament Commentary: Revelation 1-11.* (Chicago, IL: Moody, 1999), 63.

[4] Mounce, *The Book of Revelation*, 69.

[5] Lehman Strauss, *The Book of the Revelation.* (Neptune, NJ: Loizeaux, 1964), 37.

[6] Generally speaking, mission drift occurs when a church loses sight of the Great Commission and spends much of its time engaged in non-gospel tasks.

Thankfully, the Lord, in all His goodness and lovingkindness, gave the Ephesian church a corrective, though it went unheeded. But it is what is desperately needed for us to survive and thrive. He tells them, "Therefore remember from where you have fallen, and repent and do the deeds you did at first" (v. 5). While He states the consequences of disobedience in the negative, He tells them that if they commit themselves to these three things, He will spare them from having their lampstand removed. Let's look briefly at these.

First Command: Remember

When the word "remember" is used in the Bible, it often refers to the act of bringing to mind a behavior from the past and acting on it. It implies that the information needed to do the right thing exists in a memory. The way forward is, in fact, backwards. The Lord makes note that they have fallen from grace, and so, they must "remember from where [they] have fallen." In the opening chapter of this book, we examined the origins of Christianity in New England and saw it at the height of its faithfulness. From the days of the Puritans to Edwards and Whitefield to the Second Great Awakening and the advance of world missions, we have fallen like lightening! We must remember our past in order that we might return—not to the "the glory days," but to the days of faithfulness.

Second Command: Repent

The next command of Christ is to "repent"—a changing of mind for the purpose of changing one's lifestyle. This is a turning away from sin and toward obedience to the Lord. We examined this dire need in chapter 3. Unless we engage in radical repentance, the New England church will not survive the judgment of the Lord.

Third Command: Do

True repentance and faith always bear the fruit of righteousness. In the case of the Ephesians, they were to manifest "love from a pure heart and a good conscience and a sincere faith" (1 Tim. 1:5). When they stirred up true affections for Christ, their deeds became fruitful. We must do the same. With a heart devoted to Christ, we must "do the deeds [we] did at first"—loving Christ supremely, loving others selflessly, studying the Scriptures diligently, worshiping passionately, and evangelizing tirelessly.

When we examine our rich roots, it's clear that New England has lost her first love. Our heart for the Lord Jesus Christ and His gospel must be revived, and the flames of our once-burning heart must be rekindled. But how? Let's examine three basic corrective solutions.

Solution #1: Rededication

It would be easy to decry our sad departure and write-off every church in New England, but truthfully, that would be irresponsible and, frankly, sinful. Christ loves His bride and we should too! In reality, there *are* faithful churches in New England; there *is* a remnant of believers, albeit a small one (perhaps 2-3% as noted in chapter 1). But there are communities with vibrant, faithful, loving, truthful, dynamic churches who preach a saving gospel and teach the whole counsel of God.

However, since we know that pride goes before the fall (Prov. 16:18), we would do well to examine ourselves, test our motives, perform a self-check. Certainly, there are areas where even faithful churches can improve. Further, there may be churches who are running well, but have noticed sluggishness in specific areas. Maybe there are key elements that have fallen by the wayside and need to be implemented.

Pastors, maybe your love for ministry has grown cold. It's been said that New England is the pastors' graveyard—perhaps you're feeling like that's true and you'd almost rather minister somewhere "easier." It could be that your preaching has gotten mechanical, your visitation has been sparse, the gospel doesn't excite you like it once did, or your love for the people has waned. Be encouraged! You're ministering in the land of Edwards and we have the opportunity to declare the truth of Christ to a people untouched in a generation. This is tip-of-the-spear gospel work, and we are truly blessed men to be serving the Lord up here. Pray the Lord gives you a desire for Him and for His people.

Leaders, perhaps you're feeling like your work is merely business-as-usual. Where your leadership meetings used to be about outreach and ministry, now they're more about budgets and maintenance. Maybe you feel more like a slave and less like a shepherd. Rejoice! You have a high call to support your pastor and encourage the flock. The church needs strong, faithful men, and you're in a position to serve the Lord greatly in this way. Don't despise your office or think little of the work. You are stewards of the most precious people under heaven.

Church members, it's easy to feel like participation in church life is just *another* thing on your plate, and your contributions (serving, financial giving, participation, fellowship, etc.) may seem to be wearing you down. But, praise the Lord! You are the hands and feet of Christ, and the Lord has given you unique gifts to accomplish the work of ministry. Whether you're cleaning the church bathroom or sharing the gospel, you aren't just "doing ministry"—you *are* the ministers! Look for ways to encourage your pastor and leaders and serve joyfully. God will honor your faithfulness.

Churchgoers, maybe you don't darken the doors of your local church as often as you'd like. Perhaps you've been hurt in the past, or think it's not the best use of your time. Maybe you've swallowed the deadly bait of believing you can "do church" anywhere apart from the assembly of other Christians. Get in the game! The Christian life is so much richer when it is lived in fellowship with other saints. While not everything happens Sunday, it is still an important part of obeying the Lord (John 13:34-35; Heb. 10:24-25). If you're a Christian, attend regularly, pursue church membership, and look for ways to contribute. Not only will you be blessed, you will yourself be a blessing.

As we entreat the favor of the Lord, asking Him to reignite our hearts, let us strive to rededicate ourselves to Him. As we examine ourselves, let's be sure we are faithful in the right ways:

The Right Authority: Scripture

The temptation will always be to veer away from the Word of God and teach what is new, popular, or pragmatic. But we know that Scripture is fully profitable for all our needs as believers (2 Tim. 3:16-17). Further, it is the only inspired, authoritative, and inerrant source of divine revelation we have! We must be sure to build our teaching ministries firmly and squarely on Scripture, as it is how the church is nourished (Eph. 5:26-27), and the Lord has promised that it will not return to Him empty (Isa. 55:11).

The Right Message: The Gospel

The only message we can give that will save people and turn them into Christians is the gospel (Rom. 1:16). We must never shy away from declaring it boldly. Further, we must also be absolutely certain that we understand the gospel rightly. Have we watered it down? Have we changed it? Downplayed certain elements? If this is to be our message, let's be sure and get it right.

The Right Mission: Making Disciples

The Lord Jesus has charged the church with the task of making disciples (Matt. 28:19-20). The church is not a social club, a non-profit charity organization, or a political action group. Our mission is to preach to the lost, lead them to Christ, and grow them up into spiritual maturity. In the end, we must never waiver on our commitment to the Great Commission.

The Right Leadership: Elders

Jesus Christ is the head of the church (Eph. 5:23; Col. 1:18) and He never intended the church to be governed by trustees, politicians, or CEOs. The Bible is clear that God desires qualified leaders to shepherd His flock faithfully. (We will look at this more in depth in the next section.)

The Right Commitment: Membership

The church is the body of Christ (Rom. 12:4-5; 1 Cor. 12:12, 27; Eph. 4:4) and itself made up of those who have been saved by Him—Christians. Each believer is considered a member of Christ's body and must function accordingly. This is why it is so important to be sure that those who are accepted into the recognized assembly are, in fact, genuine believing Christians who are devoted to unity and service. (We will look at this more in depth in the next section.)

The Right Discipline: Christlikeness

Christians are saved by God and "predestined to be conformed to the image of [Jesus]" (Rom. 8:29). Therefore, we are to imitate Christ in every way (1 Cor. 11:1; Eph. 5:1). God's will for every believer is to be sanctified (1 Thes. 4:3)—to put off wickedness and sin, and to put on righteousness. We are never called to be haughty, legalistic, moralistic, or even religious; we are called to be holy (Matt. 5:48; 1 Pet. 1:16).

The Right Heart: Prayerful

There is no place for pride in ministry. We know that "God is opposed to the proud, but gives grace to the humble" (Jas. 4:6; cf. Prov. 3:34; 1 Pet. 5:5). A prayerful heart is a dependent heart, as well as a humble heart—a heart that will not cease to pray for God to move in the hearts of His people.

While there are countless ways for us to test ourselves in pursuit of faithfulness, even the most faithful believer will always be made aware of areas in need of improvement. Faithful churches with good bones must be continually eager to seek the Lord, praying: "Search me, O God, and know my heart; try me and know my anxious thoughts; and see if there be any hurtful way in me, and lead me in the everlasting way" (Ps. 139:23-24).

Solution #2: Revitalization

While some New England churches will do well to reassess a few key areas in order to maintain their health, there are a number of churches that are declining or dying. For some, their light will go out within a generation—when their older members pass away—while, without radical changes, other churches will be gone within a few years. But in many cases, churches suffer slow erosion prior to their death. Thom Rainer notes,

> Growth may come rapidly, but decline is usually slow, imperceptibly slow... Often the decline is in the physical facilities, but it is much more than that. The decline is in the vibrant ministries that once existed. The decline is in the prayer lives of the members who remain. The decline is in the connection with the community. The decline is in the hopes and dreams of those who remain. Decline is everywhere in the church, but many don't see it.[7]

The erosion process is often much slower in New England than in other areas of the country, as endowments keep the facilities open, thus maintaining the appearance of life. I once heard about a church

---

[7] Thom S. Rainer, *Autopsy of a Deceased Church: 12 Ways to Keep Yours Alive.* (Nashville, TN: B&H, 2014), 12-13.

in Maine that had so much money in endowments, they could never take up another offering and still pay all their bills for the next 100 years! In his experience with churches in decline, Rainer reports that "dying churches are concerned with self-preservation. They are concerned with a certain way of doing church."[8] Change is seen as the enemy, and any departure from the norm is perceived as radical and is rejected outright. But it goes deeper. "Thriving churches have the Great Commission as the center-piece of their vision," Rainer says, "while dying churches have forgotten the clear command of Christ."[9] In some cases, a church may go into self-preservation mode, being run by a few stalwart members who do nothing more than manage the endowment. At this point, their mission has been lost.

In other cases, there is a small, faithful remnant who have carried the torch, but have been unable to affect needed changes to reestablish a dynamic witness. Mike McKinley writes, "Dead churches are often populated by faithful believers who are deeply committed to their congregation. They have hung in through lean times."[10] For these beloved saints, there may not be a clear path forward, and so they simply wait for the inevitable end of their church. In all cases of churches in decline, change is needed if they are to stay afloat.

From this point forward, the prescriptions laid out in the next two sections will feel very familiar, as they have been explored throughout this book, but the goal of this chapter is to offer a few action steps that can be taken to starting down the path toward biblical faithfulness. While there may be many factors along the way that contribute to church revitalization, three main imperatives rise to the top, without which, nothing will happen at all. They are: a return to biblical authority through preaching, the implementation of godly leadership, and a focus on church membership.

Authority & Preaching

Every old church in New England has an attic full of dingy Bibles, reminiscent of a time when they were widely used. In many places,

---

[8] Ibid., 29.

[9] Ibid., 40.

[10] Mike McKinley, *Church Planting is for Wimps: How God Uses Messed-Up People to Plant Ordinary Churches That Do Extraordinary Things.* (Wheaton, IL: Crossway, 2010), 35.

Bibles are ornaments and decorations, but we must get these Bibles out of the boxes, off the display tables, and opened in the pulpits. But as we saw in chapter 2, it's not simply the act of opening or even using the Bible in the preaching, rather, it is the faithful exposition and application of God's truth that will bring about transformation.

In the end, the issue comes down to authority. Who or what has the final authority in the church? Far too often, we see church trustee boards or influential families get the final say. But this needs to end. The Bible is clear about who is in charge: Jesus Christ. Scripture calls him the chief shepherd (1 Pet 5:4). His authority is mediated to us through his Word. If a church willingly submits to the authority of Christ, there is no confusion about where the final word lies.[11]

Beyond the error of deferring to alien authorities in the church, there is the error of misunderstanding the Word itself and thereby not heeding the authority of Christ. John MacArthur notes, "One of the worst assaults on God's Word comes from people who say they believe the Bible yet don't know what it teaches."[12] But ignorance of Scripture is no excuse. New England churches need faithful pastors and preachers who can bring God's authoritative word to His people.

However, there are church growth experts who, while they would never outright deny the usefulness of the preaching of Scripture, downplay its overall significance in favor of pragmatism, growth strategies, and clever tactics. Commenting on this phenomena, David Prince notes,

It is possible that minimizing preaching in church revitalization may lead to greater short-term peace and even result in you being declared a creative, innovative leader. If so, you have your reward in full. Weak-willed preaching functions as a rhetorical narcotic on behalf of the wisdom of the world. Only a man with a blood-earnest commitment that

---

[11] Brian Croft, "Clear the Runway: Preparing Your Church for Revitalization" in R. Albert Mohler, Jr. ed., *A Guide to Church Revitalization.* (Louisville, KY: SBTS Press, 2015), 27-28.

[12] John MacArthur, *The Master's Plan for the Church.* (Chicago, IL: Moody, 2008), 24.

the word of the cross is the power of God belongs in the pulpit (1 Cor 1:18).[13]

Revitalization must begin with the faithful preaching of God's Word from New England pulpits. For this to happen, nothing more is needed than simply for the pastor to stand up in front of the assembly and begin to expound the Scriptures. It's been said that you don't need a congregational vote to change the way you preach—Amen! While this may seem like a daunting task to a pastor who is not used to preaching in this way, there are a vast number of resources available. In fact, one of the more helpful ministries aiding pastors in preaching better is the New England Center for Expository Preaching.[14]

But stated plainly, "We have to know what the Bible says about something before we can know how to act. We won't know how to worship, pray, evangelize, discipline, shepherd, train, or serve unless we know what the Word of God says."[15] Without this vital first step, all else is destined to fail. Steven Lawson has written, "If a reformation is to come to the church, it must be preceded by a reformation of the pulpit. As the pulpit goes, so goes the church."[16]

Godly Leadership

One of the more helpful books to be published in recent years on this topic is *Church Revitalization from the Inside Out* by Robert D. Stuart. His main premise is that, "Weak leaders produce weak churches, and weak churches are ineffective in reaching a dying culture with the gospel of Christ."[17] It's hard to argue against this. Despite all of the problems leading to the erosion of churches, he traces it back to one main problem: "A declining church is indicative of the great disease that is attacking the

---

[13] David E. Prince, "Lead from the Front: The Priority of Expository Preaching" in R. Albert Mohler, Jr. ed., *A Guide to Church Revitalization*. (Louisville, KY: SBTS Press, 2015), 35.

[14] www.necep.org

[15] MacArthur, *The Master's Plan for the Church*, 61.

[16] Steven J. Lawson, *Famine in the Land: A Passionate Call for Expository Preaching*. (Chicago, IL: Moody, 2003), 17.

[17] Robert D. Stuart, *Church Revitalization from the Inside Out*. (Phillipsburg, NJ: Presbyterian & Reformed, 2016), 13.

church today—poor leadership."[18] Therefore, the solution is to cultivate and appoint good leaders who will steer the church toward Christ.

However, we must examine what kinds of leaders God wants shepherding His flock. Without being overly simplistic, here are three basic markers of godly leadership.

First, church leaders must be *qualified*. They must be right for the job, qualified to lead in the church. Stuart notes, "Too commonly, however, men are nominated for office because they are known businessmen or friends of the pastor, or because they have substantial influence in the congregation."[19] This is terrible error. We cannot measure qualifications according to a worldly standard. We must appeal to Scripture. In Paul's first letter to Timothy, we read:

> "An overseer [elder]… must be above reproach, the husband of one wife, temperate, prudent, respectable, hospitable, able to teach, not addicted to wine or pugnacious, but gentle, peaceable, free from the love of money. He must be one who manages his own household well, keeping his children under control with all dignity (but if a man does not know how to manage his own household, how will he take care of the church of God?), and not a new convert, so that he will not become conceited and fall into the condemnation incurred by the devil. And he must have a good reputation with those outside the church, so that he will not fall into reproach and the snare of the devil" (1 Tim. 3:2-7; cf. Titus 1:5-9; 1 Pet. 5:1-4).

The overarching theme of elder qualification is that he is a man who is "above reproach" (vv. 2, 7). More than simply being popular in the community, he must be a man who is known for godliness and uprightness. While being "above reproach" does not mean sinless perfection, it certainly carries with it the need for a consistent track record. Dan Dumas writes,

> Being above reproach means you have unimpeachable character, but it doesn't mean you're flawless. You can't pretend you don't have weaknesses, but there's a difference between

[18] Ibid., 27.
[19] Ibid., 22.

having a bad day and having a bad year; the elder should live in such a way as to be accusation-free and without any sustained or legitimate pattern of sin.[20]

Church leaders are to manifest godly character so that they may function as examples to the flock (1 Pet. 5:3) and models of Christ-likeness to the community.

Next, church leaders must be *men*. In recent years, this issue of male leadership has become a contentious debate. In the kingdom of God, we understand that men and women have equal footing (Gal. 3:28), but the Bible and church history have proven clear on the necessity for male leadership in the office of pastor/elder (1 Tim. 3:1-2; Titus 1:5; cf. 1 Cor. 14:34-35; 1 Tim. 2:11-15).[21]

The overall lack of male leadership, especially in New England, has created a huge void that must be filled correctly. Lamenting this problem, Stuart writes,

> Men, for the most part, have abdicated their responsibility to lead, which has obligated women to fill the vacuum. Without greater male involvement, local congregations will decline into irrelevance and leadership will be relegated to women. Biblically functioning males will continue to fade from view and therefore from influence on church and family.[22]

Men must take up their mantle, dig their heels in, and lead in the church. Otherwise, the freefall will continue unimpeded.

Lastly, church leaders must *lead*. In Israel, shepherds lead their flocks from the front, they don't drive them from the rear. This is what God desires—for His shepherds to lead from the front. They must be willing to feed the sheep (John 21:15-17; 1 Pet. 5:1-4), teach sound doctrine (Titus 1:9a, 2:1) and protect the flock from false teachers (Rom. 16:17; Titus 1:9b). Godly leaders are out in front, directing believers toward Christ.

---

[20] Dan Dumas, "The Revitalizer: Who You Must Be" in R. Albert Mohler, Jr. ed., *A Guide to Church Revitalization*. (Louisville, KY: SBTS Press, 2015), 20.

[21] For a helpful understanding of the biblical teaching on men and women, see John Piper & Wayne Grudem, eds. *Recovering Biblical Manhood and Womanhood: A Response to Evangelical Feminism*. Wheaton, IL: Crossway, 2012.

[22] Stuart, *Church Revitalization*, 156-157.

When things get difficult, the tendency of leaders may be to adopt discipleship programs that promise results. Stuart warns, "Programs themselves are not bad, but when they are instituted in hopes of preventing further decay, they become millstones, pulling the church further down into oblivion."[23] Rather, church leaders are to come alongside believers and disciple them personally. This must be a prime objective: making disciples. If leaders fail to reproduce, they will inevitably stunt the growth of the church, weakening their ability to minister. In the end, we need qualified men who will lead New England churches unto faithfulness to the Lord Jesus Christ.

Church Membership

A focus on biblical preaching manifested through qualified leaders will prove utterly useless if proper church membership is neglected. While every Christian is considered a "member" of the body of Christ in a spiritual sense (1 Cor. 12:12-27), a formal commitment to the local expression of the church is absolutely essential.

The first reason for becoming a church member is to submit yourself to godly oversight. Hebrews 13:17 says, "Obey your leaders and submit to them; for they keep watch over your souls, as those who will give an account." God has appointed leaders to watch over His sheep, but they will struggle greatly to do this without a voluntary commitment to be led. In the end, this is for the spiritual care and protection of the flock.

The second reason for membership is so that believers might be able to contribute to the fellowship, utilizing their unique spiritual gifts. Mark Dever explains, "Joining a church increases our sense of ownership of the work of the church, of its community, of its budgets, of its goals. We move from being pampered consumers to becoming joyous proprietors."[24]

The third reason for seeking church membership is for the sake of church purity. So often in New England, churches are so desperate for new people, they'll welcome anyone with a pulse and a tithe check into membership regardless of their profession of faith. This is

---

[23] Ibid., 100.

[24] Dever, *Nine Marks of a Healthy Church*, 157.

terrible error! While the church is not to be an exclusive club, it certainly needs to consist of believing Christians. Otherwise, there will be a group of unregenerate people making ungodly decisions, accepting false doctrine, and bringing a reproach to the name of Christ in the community. A healthy process for church membership will help ensure that those who identify with the body of Christ are those who truly belong to Him. Mark Dever is convinced that "getting this concept of membership right is a key step in revitalizing our churches, evangelizing our nation, furthering the cause of Christ around the world, and so bringing glory to God."[25]

But what if the church is too far gone? What if the members are too resistant? Mike McKinley keenly notes, "It's not easy to find a church that's interested in being revitalized. Often the church is dead or almost dead because the outlaws took control. They're not looking for a sheriff to come in and clean up their mess."[26] In these cases, the wisest thing to do for the kingdom is to allow these outlaw churches to fade out, and begin a new work.

Solution #3: Church Planting

I'm convinced that church planting has a lot more to do with "church" than it does "planting." In order to be an effective church planter, you must have a robust ecclesiology. After all, beginning a new work—a local expression of the body of Christ—is not a separate Christian mission; it *is* the mission. The gospel call goes out to all people in every region, and where there is no gospel, there can be no church. Thus, when people are saved in a new area, a new church arises. And the work of the church planter is to spearhead this new work, bringing the gospel and Christian ministry to unreached areas. As we saw at the beginning of this book, New England is replete with areas where there is no gospel witness, and we are considered to be an unreached people group. Therefore, church planting is absolutely vital.

Of the writing of church planting books, there is no end. These days, it seems that every church strategist has a trademarked method on how to plant a successful church. Further, many of them make it

---

[25] Ibid., 148.
[26] McKinley, *Church Planting is for Wimps*, 34.

seem like if you don't follow their 30-step process, your church will fail in the first five years! But the Bible affirms that it is Christ who builds His church (Matt. 16:18) and even a perfect storm of procedural mistakes will not prevail against it.

Bottom line: If God wants a church to be planted, it will get planted. And if He wants it to survive, it will survive. However, there still exists a series of factors that must exist for a church to be planted and take root. Thankfully, those essential elements are spelled out on the ancient pages of Scripture.

Early Church Planting

Jesus was the original church planter. He had told the disciples that He would build the church (Matt. 16:18), He established the first church (Acts 2:1-11), and He continues to grow the church (1 Cor. 3:7). He loves the church as a bride, nourishing her and cherishing her (Eph. 5:25-27). In seeking to imitate the Lord in every way, the first believers manifested a love for the church and sought to see it grow and expand to all regions of the earth, as the Lord had promised (Acts 1:8).

While there is no explicit command in Scripture to plant churches, the practice itself is inherent as the gospel spreads and new believers gather together. In Jerusalem, the church swelled in size as "the Lord was adding to their number day by day those who were being saved" (Acts 2:47; cf. 5:14, 6:7). However, when persecution arose against the church, "[the believers] were all scattered throughout the regions of Judea and Samaria" (Acts 8:1). As the gospel went out to unreached cities and towns, new churches began to sprout up all over the Palestinian region. But it wasn't until a man named Paul encountered the Lord on the road to Damascus that the gospel would expand to the whole known world.

From the time he was called into ministry in Acts 13, the apostle Paul, along with other companions, would set out on three missionary journeys, establishing churches as he went. In fact, Paul labored to plant churches in cities such as Iconium (Acts 14:1-5), Lystra (Acts 14:6-20), Derbe (Acts 14:20-21), Philippi (Acts 16:11-40), Thessalonica (Acts 17:1-4), Berea (Acts 17:10-12), Corinth (Acts 18:1-17), Ephesus (Acts 18:23-19:41), as well as Colossae and Cenchrea, amongst others. Not only did he plant various churches personally, but Paul also trained up and sent out other church planters and ministry leaders, such as Timothy, Priscilla and Aquila, Apollos, Epaphras, and Titus.

Titus: The Ancient Church Planter's Manual

While the biblical data is clear that churches were indeed planted, there is no explicit record of how they were planted. However, we do have a brief letter sent to one of Paul's closest disciples, Titus, outlining the basic approach needed to establish churches on the island of Crete.

The letter is short—only 46 verses—but it highlights for us what Paul likely spent years teaching his young disciple in the ministry. Titus had the daunting task of reorganizing what was there and planting where needed. Paul specifically told him, "For this reason I left you in Crete, that you might set in order what remains, and appoint elders in every city as I directed you" (Titus 1:5). The letter would serve as a guide for the work he was about to do. In his commentary on the Epistle to Titus, Daniel Akin writes, "We could consider the theme [of Titus] to be 'An Apostolic Manual for Church Planting.' Here is a blueprint for planting and building churches that will survive and thrive for the glory of God."[27] With nearly a hundred cities on Crete, Titus would need a duplicable process. The principles gleaned from this epistle are no doubt essential elements needed in church planting.

First, *identify the mission*. It is curious that Paul includes such a lengthy greeting for such a short letter, but the purpose is clear. Paul is establishing not only his authority as an apostle, but also the mission that is being assigned to Titus. Paul writes that his ministry is "for the faith of those chosen of God and the knowledge of the truth which is according to godliness, in the hope of eternal life" (Titus 1:1b-2a). Many commentators have noted three key aspects to Paul's mission:

1. Leading people to faith in Christ;
2. Teaching believers to live godly; and
3. Giving believers hope for the future.

---

[27] Daniel L. Akin, "Titus" in David Platt, Daniel L. Akin, and Tony Merida, *Christ-Centered Exposition: 1 & 2 Timothy and Titus.* (Nashville, TN: B&H, 2013), 226.

While the ministry is multi-faceted, Paul kept his eyes focused on the most important elements—those pertaining to justification, sanctification, and glorification.

Second, *appoint elders.* Much like in 1 Timothy 3, Paul gives the required qualifications for elders in Titus 1:6-9. As a pastor bearing Paul's delegated apostolic authority, Titus would have to identify qualified Christian men and appoint them into leadership. Even today, we need qualified leaders in church planting. While some churches are launched through the efforts of a qualified core team, a few elders, or a sole planting pastor, the imperative for leaders who meet biblical qualifications is key.

Third, *establish discipleship.* While Titus 1 is focused heavily on the ministry of the leaders, chapter 2 focuses on the ministry of the body. Not only does Paul point to the need for church members to learn sound doctrine (2:1), they must also live it out (2:2-10). Further, the mandate for discipleship reaches the whole church—older men and women, younger women and men. No one is exempt. Discipleship was essential for the churches on Crete; it is no less essential for every modern church plant as well.

Fourth, *devote yourselves to outreach.* While we know that the body of Christ is supposed to build itself up in maturity (cf. Eph. 4:12-16), there is the ever-present danger of becoming too inwardly focused. That's why Paul tells Titus, "I want you to speak confidently, so that those who have believed God may be careful to engage in good deeds. These things are good and profitable for men" (3:8). Several times in the letter, Paul places an emphasis on "good deeds" (vv. 2:7, 14, 3:8, 14) for the purpose of blessing others. This is not our natural focus, nor was it theirs, which is why he instructs Titus to "let our people also learn to engage in good deeds to meet pressing needs, that they may not be unfruitful" (3:14). After all, the Lord Jesus Christ has redeemed and purified "a people for His own possession [who are] zealous for good deeds" (2:14). In order to make the gospel attractive to unbelievers (2:10), the church must have an outward focus of good deeds.

With the space provided in this book, there is no way to provide instruction on every nuance of church planting, but there are many other resources available.[28] However, when contemplating the possibility of planting in New England, we need to see that the required elements for biblical faithfulness in church planting are no farther away than the Bible itself.

Reasons to Plant Churches in New England

There are always arguments against church planting which I won't exhaust here. While some arguments are valid, and there are certainly cases when church planting may be inappropriate,[29] I firmly believe New England to be a region in desperate need of new churches. Here are just a few reasons:

First, the number of gospel-preaching churches is very small. It may be hard to believe, but there are whole towns and regions where there are no churches who actively preach the gospel. Geographically speaking, the gospel is absent, and in some places, whole communities have not heard the gospel preached in decades.

Second, the number of Bible-teaching churches is very small. Even if a church may present the gospel once in awhile, it is exceedingly rare to find a ministry that teaches the whole counsel of God. Simply finding a church in New England that will faithfully teach the Bible is a rarity.

Third, new churches can reach people not reached by existing churches. Historically, New England is the oldest region in America, and there are many churches in the Northeast that are several hundred years old. Over time, a church may lose its witness and the locals simply aren't keen to listen. A new church may appeal to those curious, and may be zealous and evangelistic enough to work harder to win people over to Christ.

Fourth, new churches are needed to help saturate the region. In my humble estimation, each town needs 3-5 new churches sim-

---

[28] Many helpful resources include: Craig Ott and Gene Wilson, *Global Church Planting: Biblical Principles and Best Practices for Multiplication*. Grand Rapids, MI: Baker, 2011; and David J. Hesselgrave, *Planting Churches Cross-Culturally: North American and Beyond*. Grand Rapids, MI: Baker, 2000.

[29] Generally, a new church plant is needed where there is no gospel witness. However, in towns with already present gospel-preaching churches, discernment is needed. In some cases, it might actually be better to partner with the existing church.

ply to match the population density. With Bible-believing Christians making up only 2-3% of New England, there are simply not enough churches and resources to accommodate the large numbers of people should the Spirit work and add them to the church. More churches can get the gospel out and make provision for those who are coming into the body of Christ.

Fifth, new churches bring a level of excitement and vitality to a spiritually cold region. Church planters are generally more zealous to fulfill the Great Commission and will tend to go farther to reach the lost. This excitement can be contagious, and we need more strong believers with deep affections for Christ who will maintain a fervent witness. Again, some communities have never experienced a vibrant church full of believers who are in love with Jesus Christ.

Sixth, more churches means less travel for churchgoers and more opportunity for community involvement. The practical considerations must be on the forefront of our minds. It is not uncommon for believers to endure long commutes, often feeling disconnected from the local church community. If believers could worship and serve in a body in their own town or area, their commitment would naturally increase and ministry would become more effective. This would establish firmer foundations in each local area.

Where Do We Go From Here?

At this point, the task might seem overwhelming. With such a large amount of territory and so many unsaved people, how does one even begin this work? Before any sermon can be preached, or any church planted, the work must begin on our knees.

7

THE HARVEST IS PLENTIFUL, BUT—

About ten minutes from my home is the Alton Bay Christian Conference Center. It's a beautiful piece of wooded property couched on a mountainside overlooking Lake Winnipesaukee. The Center has been there since the mid-1800s and was once a popular stop along the railway line. In the summertime, more than 20,000 people would arrive on the grounds for revival meetings, and listen to some of the greatest preachers of the day. But those days are gone. While the Center is still in use, the bustling glory days are likely far behind us.

I've often thought about what revival might look like in the Northeast, but I'm pretty sure it won't consist of big tent meetings like during the Second Great Awakening. There are several reasons for this. First, the times have changed and people don't flock to Crusade-like events like they used to. Second, history has proven that true lasting revival does not take place through big event gatherings, but through the consistent fellowship of the local church. And so, I've grown to believe that revival in New England will look different.

Dream with me for a minute. Imagine a Bible church in every town in New England–large and small. Christians would no longer need to drive 20, 30, or 40 miles to find a church that teaches sound doctrine; there would be one in their hometown. The majority of church members would be local, and therefore, ready and able to minister to their neighbors. With a stronger local expression, the depth of ministry would deepen and lasting witness could be maintained. While the cities would certainly have larger churches, the majority of smaller towns would have smaller congregations of less than a few hundred.

However, with all of the territorial bases covered, the expansion of the gospel would be far reaching, and would slowly boil up, overflowing to every square inch of the region. With deep, healthy gospel roots in every town, future generations wouldn't need to replant and recover what was lost; they could continue to build. And by the grace of God, New England could become a light to the nations once again!

How might this happen? Larger coordinated efforts are difficult to get off the ground and existing congregations are already stretched thin. A new strategy is needed.

Actually, it's an old strategy.

The Nehemiah Strategy

While we cannot hope to return to the Awakening days of early New England, we should certainly seek to be faithful to God in the ways of our spiritual fathers. At the risk of sounding too pragmatic, it must be said that what we're doing up here isn't working.

When the Israelites returned from seventy years of Babylonian exile, they found Jerusalem in ruins. Cyrus the Persian king had decreed that the city should be rebuilt (Ezra 1:1-4), and eventually Nehemiah was appointed to the task of overseeing the work (Neh. 2:1-5). The strategy was simple: every man would focus on building the wall that was in front of his own house, and when that was completed, he would help others (3:1-32). While their enemies were opposing them heavily, threatening their lives and their work, the Israelites labored on. After fifty-two days, the city wall was completed, and Nehemiah wrote, "And it came about when all our enemies heard of it, and the nations surrounding us saw it, they lost their confidence; for they recognized that this work had been accomplished with the help of our God" (Neh. 6:16).

Much like the faithful small-town pastors of the First and Second Great Awakenings, we need laborers who will focus their energy on building the wall that is in front of them. If every town had a gospel-preaching, Bible-teaching church led by competent pastors and leaders, laboring tirelessly for as long as it took, the whole region would soon be inundated, and the Christian witness would be incalculable. If men would dig in, working shoulder-to-shoulder, the work needed to advance the kingdom of Christ would get done, and it would be built on solid rock!

Of course, this monumental feat cannot be accomplished in the arm of the flesh.

The Lord of the Harvest

While He was still on earth, the Lord Jesus was appointing and sending His disciples to preach the gospel of the kingdom to the people in cities where He was about to travel. Prior to their departure, He was telling them, "The harvest is plentiful, but the laborers are few; therefore beseech the Lord of the harvest to send out laborers into His harvest" (Luke 10:2). Jesus knew the work was vast and the challenges would be great, but He commanded them to trust the Lord and look to Him for the needed help.

In the Northeast, it is much the same. The number of unreached people is staggering, and there are so few believers for the work. The task seems daunting, but we know that the Lord is the One who owns and oversees the harvest fields. If we desire revival, our own efforts will produce nothing if divorced from the Spirit. In obedience to His command, we must beseech the Lord of the harvest.

We must manifest a radical dependence on God. We must pray constantly (1 Thes. 5:17). We must pray earnestly (Col. 4:2). We must beseech the Lord of the harvest, begging Him to send laborers, and to save lost souls. After all, salvation does not come through the will of man, but by the will of God (John 1:12-13). God must act, therefore we must pray.

A Surprising Work of the Spirit

As we have seen, revival is never something that can be man-made, rather, as the Puritans bore witness, it is a surprising work of the Spirit of God. Therefore, we must entreat the Lord of the harvest. We must pray earnestly that He might open blind eyes, unstop deaf ears, and ignite cold hearts.

Faithful believers, pray for New England! Ask the Lord to raise up pastors, preachers, disciple-makers, workers, and servants. Ask the Lord to send Bible expositors and church planters and evangelists.

Body of Christ, recommit your way to the Lord! Bear fruits worthy of repentance and faith. Devote yourselves to godliness. Put off lethargy, apathy, indifference, pride, and ungodliness; put on godliness, truthfulness, love, and joy.

New England saints, labor faithfully! Ingest the Word of God, know His precepts, preach the saving gospel of Jesus Christ, and do good works that bear witness to Him.

And if God so wills to work through our obedience, He just may revive New England.

APPENDIX

WHEN THE REFORMATION CAME TO NEW ENGLAND

This article was first published on EntreatingFavor.com (2/4/16) as the first of a series of articles written in preparation for Reviving New England.

When most people think of the Protestant Reformation, their minds often latch onto the image of Martin Luther nailing his 95 *Theses* to the door of the castle at Wittenberg on October 31, 1517. From there, other names such as Calvin, Beza, Knox, and Zwingli are not too far behind. But what if I were to tell you that the Protestant Reformation had a strong and vibrant surge on the shores of America in the seventeenth century? Most Christian history textbooks all but forget the most radical of Reformers who fled persecution and settled in Plymouth, Massachusetts in the 1620s and 1630s.

In the wake of the Reformation, Europe had its hands full, trying to figure out what to do with the religious upheaval. Almost immediately, war erupted as the Roman Catholic Church lunged at the Reformers to snuff out the resistance and maintain control, but very quickly it became apparent that different measures were needed.

When a very Roman Catholic Queen Mary I came to power in 1553, she immediately lashed out at Protestantism, martyring 283 believers in 1555. But by 1560, Queen Elizabeth I had ascended the throne and worked to provide toleration for the dissenting Protestants. At this time, she established "the Elizabethan Compromise" which would draw together "Reformed or Calvinistic *doctrine*, the continuation of a liturgical and... Catholic *form of worship*, and an episcopal *church government*."[1] Essentially, this move was designed to keep all parties happy, but the Puritan Reformers would have nothing of it. They were committed not only to *reform* the church, but also *purify* the church of the remaining elements of Roman Catholic liturgy and dogma.

But this task of purification was proving to be nearly impossible. Some of the English preachers were so unskilled and ignorant, others so puffed up and pretentious—they could barely lead the congregation in any sort of way of godliness. Historian Edmund S. Morgan notes,

> In England, they said, too many ministers substituted an affected eloquence for sound knowledge and indulged themselves 'in [fond] fables to make their hearers [laugh], or in ostentation of learning of their Latin, their [Greek], their [Hebrew] tongue, and of their great reading of antiquities.' Worse than these dilettante preachers were the ignorant and evil ministers, incapable of preaching at all.[2]

Not only were the ministers awful, but the corruption in the church was prevalent. Regardless of one's behavior, church membership was nearly freely granted, and since all disciplinary power was maintained solely by the bishops, there was no way for a church to rid themselves of sinning members. Therefore, church purification was impossible.

With no way for Puritans to reform the Church of England, many had no choice but to separate.

But the English Separatists were not simply able to dodge the Church of England at ease. Even the renowned King James I vowed to force the Puritans to conform or else he would "harry them out of the land."[3] The Separatists were despised by their English countrymen, oppressed and derided. And for one congregation, the time to act was now.

---

[1] Leland Ryken, *Worldly Saints: The Puritans As They Really Were.* (Grand Rapids, MI: Zondervan, 1986), 7. Italics original.

[2] Edmund S. Morgan, *Visible Saints: The History of the Puritan Idea.* (New York, NY: New York University Press, 1963), 7.

[3] B.K. Kuiper, *The Church in History.* (Grand Rapids, MI: Eerdmans, 1951), 327.

In 1609, a group of Puritan Separatists in Scrooby, England decided to flee to Holland. Very quickly they realized that life was not much better there, and their children were still being exposed to the same revelry they found in England. And so, finally, they decided to set sail for the New World.

Most American schoolchildren grew up learning about the voyage of the Mayflower across impossible seas, landing at Plymouth Rock in 1620. We heard about their difficult first winter, the death of nearly half the settlers, and the first Thanksgiving that followed once they had made contact with the native inhabitants. We know the stories; they seem almost like fairy tales to us now. But what was it that drove them to endure such hardship in fleeing England and Holland, braving the North Atlantic, and suffering tumultuous New England winters?

Purity of worship.

The Puritan believers were not just disciplined, they were also devoted. They valued good preaching, sound doctrine, holy living, and discipleship. The Church of England, even though technically "Protestant" in designation, still did not value faithfulness, righteousness, and individual soul liberty. Much of English religion was politicized. The fires of Reformation had simmered down to lukewarm coals. And while many migrated to America in the early 1600s for many reasons, many residents writing back to England argued that "the only valid reason for migrating to Massachusetts was religion."[4] In short, the Puritans' primary focus was to establish "pure" churches.

All of the best elements of the Reformation—sound doctrine, biblical preaching, church purity, education, the priesthood of all believers—these were the sought after elements in their striving for "pure" churches.

For a short season, the New England Puritans attained what they were striving for. While they failed to create "New Jerusalem" on American shores, they succeeded in creating a society that embraced Christianity.

However, this micro-utopia would not last.

---

[4] Everett Emerson, *Puritanism in America: 1620-1750*. (Boston, MA: Twayne, 1977), 32.

FOR FURTHER READING ON EARLY AMERICAN CHRISTIANITY AND REVIVAL

Leland Ryken. *Worldly Saints: The Puritans As They Really Were.* Grand Rapids, MI: Zondervan, 1986.

Everett Emerson. *Puritanism in America 1620-1750.* Boston, MA: Twayne, 1977.

Thomas S. Kidd. *The Great Awakening: The Roots of Evangelical Christianity in Colonial America.* New Haven, CT: Yale, 2007.

Iain H. Murray. *Revival and Revivalism: The Making and Marring of American Evangelicalism 1750-1858.* Edinburgh: Banner of Truth, 1994.

Iain H. Murray. *Pentecost-Today? The Biblical Basis for Understanding Revival.* Edinburgh: Banner of Truth, 1998.

Walter C. Kaiser, Jr. *Revive Us Again: Biblical Principles for Revival Today.* Fearn, Scotland: Christian Focus, 2001.

For more information about
HARVEST BIBLE CHURCH

Go to: **www.harvestbiblegilmanton.org**

Also, be sure to visit **www.EntreatingFavor.com**

and

www.Servantsofgrace.org

Please visit:

The New England Center for Expository Preaching

(www.necep.org)

Made in United States
Orlando, FL
20 August 2022